ROSENWALD COLLECTION
REPRINT SERIES

THE DANCE OF DEATH
by Hans Holbein the Younger

A Complete Facsimile of the Original 1538 Edition of
Les simulachres & historiees faces de la mort, with a
new introduction by Werner L. Gundersheimer

A BRIEFE AND TRUE REPORT OF THE NEW
FOUND LAND OF VIRGINIA
by Thomas Harriot

The complete 1590 Theodor de Bry edition, with a new
introduction by Paul Hulton

A BRIEFE AND TRUE REPORT OF
THE NEW FOUND LAND OF VIRGINIA

Thomas Harriot

A BRIEFE AND TRUE REPORT OF THE NEW FOUND LAND OF VIRGINIA

THE COMPLETE 1590 THEODOR DE BRY EDITION

With a new Introduction by

Paul Hulton

Assistant Keeper, Department of Prints and Drawings

The British Museum

Dover Publications, Inc., New York

Published in Canada by General Publishing Company, Ltd., 30 Lesmill Road, Don Mills, Toronto, Ontario.
Published in the United Kingdom by Constable and Company, Ltd., 10 Orange Street, London WC 2.

This Dover edition, first published in 1972, is an unabridged republication of the English-language version of the first illustrated edition of the work, originally published by Theodor de Bry (printed by Johann Wechel) in 1590 at Frankfurt a/M. The work has been reproduced from the Library of Congress (Rosenwald) copy.

A new Introduction has been written specially for the present edition by Paul Hulton; there is a new Publisher's Note; and five illustrations of original drawings by White and Le Moyne have been added.

International Standard Book Number: 0-486-21092-8
Library of Congress Catalog Card Number: 79-179788

Manufactured in the United States of America
Dover Publications, Inc.
180 Varick Street
New York, N. Y. 10014

Publisher's Note

The present unabridged republication of the first illustrated edition of Harriot's *Briefe and true report* is reproduced from the copy that Mr. Lessing J. Rosenwald has presented to the Library of Congress. To obtain the best results, a few of the plates were reproduced from the French-language edition (issued simultaneously with the English edition), also in Mr. Rosenwald's collection. Without the kind cooperation of Mr. Rosenwald, the Dover edition would not have been possible. This volume is the second in a series of Dover reprints of great rare books from the Rosenwald Collection at the Alverthorpe Gallery, Jenkintown, Pennsylvania. This series is an important extension of the Gallery's continuing program of art education and scholarship.

INTRODUCTION
to the Dover Edition

THOMAS HARRIOT first published his *Briefe and true report of the new found land of Virginia* in 1588 as a modest quarto volume without illustrations; it is now one of the rarest of Americana. Two years later, in 1590, appeared Theodor de Bry's folio edition, with illustrations by John White, issued separately in four languages—Latin, English, French and German—which followed one another within the space of days and constituted the first part of *America,* De Bry's series of volumes on the discovery of the New World. The present volume reproduces the English version of that celebrated work.

The English had arrived late in the field of North American exploration and settlement in spite of the brilliant early start provided by the expeditions of the Cabots. They had been slow to follow these up, confining their activities to the Newfoundland fishing grounds and the attempts by Frobisher in the late 1570's to discover the supposed northwest route to Asia. Only in the next decade had the impetus grown sufficiently strong for the first attempt at settlement to be made. This owed much to Sir Walter Raleigh's powerful position as promoter and financial backer. In 1584 Amadas and Barlowe explored the eastern coast of North America in the area of the Carolina Outer Banks, called Virginia in honor of Queen Elizabeth, who granted Raleigh a patent to settle there. They brought back invaluable information about the Indians (and produced two live ones) and the physical characteristics of the country as well as an over-optimistic report of its economic possibilities for settlement. In July 1585 began the first major attempt under Sir Richard Grenville, with Ralph Lane as Governor, to establish a colony on Roanoke Island, off the coast explored in 1584. After twelve months the venture failed for the same basic reasons as had earlier French efforts in Florida and others before them; the colonists found it impossible to remain self-sufficient and, facing a shortage of supplies, chose to be transported back to England by Drake, who was returning from his West Indian voyage. There was naturally a considerable degree of disillusionment which Raleigh felt it essential to combat if further expeditions were to succeed. Harriot's *Briefe and true report* was conceived at this moment and seems to have found its final form a year later when a fresh attempt to plant a colony was under way. Raleigh's hopes had been somewhat dimmed by the turn of events and he had delegated the task of founding a settlement to a company headed by John White, the recording artist of the previous expedition, who was appointed Governor of the new colony. His fleet got to sea in April 1587, but instead of settling in Chesapeake Bay, as White intended, a near mutiny forced him to return to the Island of Roanoke. As a leader White was undoubtedly less effective than as an artist. After a surprisingly short time he returned to England for supplies, leaving behind him his daughter Eleanor, with her husband Ananias Dare and their newly born child Virginia. Raleigh was sympathetic and promised further help but by the spring of 1588 the Armada was threatening and all plans for a major relief expedition had to be abandoned. Now, too late for its main purpose, Harriot's *Report* was published. Had it appeared before White had begun to assemble his expedition of 1587 it might have had a more useful effect. For its main aim was to attract settlers and investors in a venture which seemed to promise rich rewards. This Harriot set out to demonstrate by a careful survey of the economic possibilities of the new land and its natural resources. But by the time the book appeared White's return and the extreme difficulties facing the colony would have become general knowledge. He was not able to reach Roanoke Island again until August 1590 when he found the site of the colony deserted. Though there were signs that the colonists had left for the Island of Croatoan the search had to be abandoned and from that moment the Lost Colony moves into legend. This was the final collapse of the efforts begun in 1584 to establish an English foothold on the North American continent. Only a short time before that sombre moment De Bry had republished Harriot's optimistic assessment of the colony in Virginia, this time with White's illustrations to Harriot's additional notes on the Indians. But now the emphasis had shifted. Though the text of that propagandist tract remained unrevised, the illustrations with the notes and the map impressively emphasized the scientific, in particular the ethnological, discoveries of the English in Virginia. This aspect of the book is even further enhanced by the high quality of the engraved plates.

Of the two main authors of the De Bry volume surprisingly little is known. Thomas Harriot was the outstanding English scientist and mathematician of his time, yet his scientific work remained unpublished during his lifetime and little has appeared since. Now, three hundred and fifty years after his death, serious efforts are at last being made to publish his papers. He was born in Oxford in 1560, in the parish of St Mary, and in 1577 became a student at St Mary's Hall in the University. After graduating he joined the household of Sir Walter Raleigh as tutor in the "mathematical sciences"—which is likely to have meant astronomy and navigation. It is not difficult to imagine that these studies acted as a stimulus to Raleigh's concern with overseas exploration. Raleigh inherited his half-brother Sir Humphrey Gilbert's interest in North American exploration and settlement but, whereas Gilbert's schemes had been amateurish in practice, Raleigh's, with the advantage of Harriot's expertise, promised to be as professional in their realization as in their planning. In 1584 Harriot drew up instructions on navigation for Amadas and Barlowe's reconnaissance, which carried out its mission most effectively though Harriot himself was not present. He was, however, a member of

Grenville's expedition of 1585–6. His duties were to make astronomical observations, advise on navigation for the voyage and, on land, in close cooperation with John White, to study the native Indians and natural products of the country as well as to supervise the mapping of the new territories. There is no doubt that the two carried through their tasks in considerable detail and with an unusual degree of scientific method. It must surely have been Harriot's ability to control the cartographical survey by astronomical observations, employing a uniform scale, which accounted for the unprecedented accuracy of White's maps, at least of the area which the Englishmen themselves explored. Of the extent of the survey of natural life we get some inkling from occasional clues in the text, as: "Of al sorts of fowle I haue the names in the countrie language of fourescore and sixe of which number besides those that be named, we haue . . . the pictures as they were there drawne . . . ." Of Harriot's "Chronicle," which we know he compiled during his time with the colony, nothing remains but an abstract—the *Report*. Yet relics of the major survey still survive in John White's natural history drawings (originals and copies) at the British Museum. Harriot states his intention in the *Report* to publish this natural history material (p. 20) but, for reasons which are not clear, none of it was included in the De Bry folio.

Harriot seems to have had a special responsibility for studying the native Indians, and possibly he himself looked upon this as the most important aspect of his work. From Manteo and Wanchese, the Indians captured by Amadas and Barlowe, he may have made a study of the Algonkian language, for some of his papers on this subject were still extant in 1684. Information about Harriot after his involvement in the Virginia enterprise is meagre. In about 1590 he was introduced by Raleigh to Henry, ninth Earl of Northumberland, who became his patron, allowing him a life pension. After the Earl's imprisonment in the Tower in 1606, he granted Harriot a residence at Syon House, Isleworth, where he continued his studies. Even as early as this, in correspondence with Kepler on optical problems, Harriot mentions his inability to write or even think accurately on any subject. In spite of this he seems to have achieved much scientific work before his death, of cancer of the nose, in 1621.

Of the second author of the De Bry volume, John White, much less is known except for his part in the Roanoke voyages. It is likely that he was born between 1540 and 1550 and came from a West Country family. Eskimo studies in the British Museum by and after White support the theory that he sailed as recording artist with Frobisher on his second expedition of 1577. He was probably the John White who was recorded in 1580 as a member of the Painter-Stainers' Company of London, but the first definite record of him is in 1585, when he was named as one of Grenville's party which explored the coast of Pamlico Sound, though there is indirect evidence that he first sailed with Amadas and Barlowe in 1584. After his failure to find the colonists in 1590 nothing more of White is heard,

Fig. 1: Indians dancing. Original drawing by John White; see Plate XVIII. (Courtesy Trustees of the British Museum)

Fig. 2: "One of their Religious men." Original drawing by John White; see Plate V. (Courtesy Trustees of the British Museum)

Fig. 3: "A cheife Herowans wyfe of Pomeoc and her daughter of the age of 8 or 10 yeares." Original drawing by John White; see Plate VIII. (Courtesy Trustees of the British Museum)

except in 1593, when he wrote to Richard Hakluyt from Raleigh's estate in Ireland, enclosing the account of his last voyage. No record of his death has so far been discovered.

We have no idea what training as an artist White received but he certainly possessed precisely the kind of graphic ability required—a quick eye and hand which complemented Harriot's analytical method. In addition to his Indian material he must have made many hundreds of drawings of every kind in the field— maps, topography, birds, beasts, reptiles, fishes and plants—and those which survive give us a clear idea of his range and skills. He worked speedily with the capacity to put on record every kind of detail required. The engravings will be seen to be generally faithful to the originals though De Bry often Europeanizes his Indian faces and postures. The engraving of the Indians dancing (Plate XVIII) makes an instructive comparison with the original drawing (Fig. 1); De Bry's tendency to idealize the features and soften the more awkward gestures is evident. White's portrait studies are engagingly straightforward (Figs. 2-4). It will be observed that the engraver was using other versions of White's originals,

Fig. 4: "Theire sitting at meate." Original drawing by John White; see Plate XVI. (Courtesy Trustees of the British Museum)

which, though basically the same as those now surviving, often included much additional detail (cf. Plates V, VIII and XVI).

Probably at about the time that White first became involved in the Virginia ventures, he met the French artist Jacques Le Moyne de Morgues. Le Moyne had anticipated almost exactly White's role as recording artist, having accompanied Laudonnière on the Florida expedition of 1563–5. He escaped the savage massacre by which the Spaniards had put an end to French hopes of establishing a Protestant colony there. By the early 1580's he had settled in England "for religion." There was clearly an interchange of material and ideas between White and the older artist and this fact has some bearing on the curious set of "Picts" which follow the Indians in the illustrated *Report*. They were added, De Bry says, by White to show "how that the Inhabitants of the great Bretannie haue bin in times past as sauuage as those of Virginia." But a drawing by Le Moyne has recently appeared (Fig. 5) which seems to be the original of the young Pictish woman (Picts, Plate III). Was Le Moyne the originator of all these figures and did White copy them from him?

Fig. 5: Young Pictish woman. Original drawing by Jacques Le Moyne de Morgues; see Plate III of the section on Picts. (Courtesy Paul Mellon, Upperville, Va.)

The part of the Flemish engraver and publisher Theodor de Bry in the planning and production of the illustrated *Report* was a major one. He was in England in 1587 attempting to acquire Le Moyne's Florida narrative and illustrations but the artist was unwilling to sell. On a second visit, probably late in 1588, soon after Le Moyne's death, he was successful in buying them from his widow. But he seems to have been persuaded by Richard Hakluyt (and by his own admiration of White's drawings) to publish the Harriot-White material first as the first part of his projected *America*. The multilingual edition was decided on, a source of pride to Harriot, and the eminent botanist Charles de l'Écluse, was commissioned to translate Harriot's English into both Latin and French. Raleigh no doubt gave the work his blessing and De Bry dedicated the book to him, "seeing that . . . VIRGINIA hath ben descouuered by yours meanes."

The De Bry edition of the *Report* is the first of its kind which can justifiably be described as scientific in both text and illustration. That is not to say that it is entirely objective or free from wishful thinking, but the approach and method are factual and analytical, the mood is restrained, and when over-sanguine conclusions are drawn they are at least based on evidence which is carefully considered. Harriot presents only the subject matter which concerns the economic viability of the colony and its future prospects; the Indians could be thought of as aiding or obstructing that end and their way of life needed careful study. He pays close attention to their economy but says almost nothing about their social and political organization. Above all he is interested in their religion and the favorable impact of Protestant Christianity on the savage mind. White's illustrations are largely confined to the Indian way of life: their villages, agriculture, crafts, dress, cooking and eating, fishing and ceremonies, which are portrayed with unprecedented realism. The illustrated *Report* is therefore a source of the greatest value for our understanding of the extinct Southeastern Algonkians—and where archeological evidence is available, it almost invariably supports the accuracy of Harriot's and White's observations.

None of the earlier sixteenth-century publications on the American discoveries approach the De Bry volume in scientific accuracy or graphic realism. Gonzalo Fernández de Oviedo, author of a "natural y general hystoria de las Indias," had something of Harriot's approach, revolutionary at this early period, but lacked, he says, a Michelangelo or a Leonardo to portray what he could not express in words, and the published forms of the work are without effective illustrations. The woodcuts in Jean de Léry's *Histoire d'un voyage fait en la terre du Bresil* (1578) are superior but his handling of the ethnological discoveries of Villégaignon's colony of 1555 is limited. He complains of the problem of portraying "these barbarian people" inasmuch as "by reason of their diverse gestures and behaviors, utterly different from ours, it is a very difficult matter to express their true proportion, either in writing or painting." Harriot and particularly White were able to do precisely that.

One illustrated survey of the New World might well have rivaled that of Harriot and White. It was made by Francisco Hernández for Philip II, with the help of a team of painters and collectors of specimens and a cartographer which he had assembled in Mexico from 1571 to 1577. The notes and drawings filled fifteen large manuscript volumes but they were destroyed by fire in the Escorial in 1671.

The French efforts to establish themselves in Florida in the 1560's produced valuable accounts by Ribault, Laudonnière and others which throw much light on the Timucua Indians of the St Johns River but they are unsystematic and unillustrated. Only the illustrated narrative of the colony of 1564–5 by Jacques Le Moyne de Morgues can be compared with the De Bry edition of the *Report*. The text, however, is in no sense a scientific survey but a rather rambling account. The forty-two plates, with notes, and the map are far less precise or reliable than their White-Harriot counterparts, no doubt because Le Moyne was unable to salvage enough of his graphic records and sometimes invents where he cannot reconstruct.

Harriot's *Report* was included in Richard Hakluyt's famous *Principal navigations* (both the editions of 1589 and 1598–1600) without White's illustrations, but De Bry's edition of 1590 had the deepest and most lasting influence. Harriot's observations and White's figures reappear, sometimes in light disguise, in early writings on Virginia, and the engravings of De Bry after White are frequently found in modified form in works of comparative ethnology as typifying the North American Indian until far into the eighteenth century. In these late works the writers of the Age of Enlightenment showed themselves less scientific than their models, for by their time the Southeastern Algonkians, whom Harriot and White so carefully observed, had as a distinct culture disappeared.

PAUL HULTON

Suggestions for Further Reading

Books containing useful information on the historical background to the colonizing enterprises in Raleigh's Virginia and the personalities involved:

A. L. Rowse, *Sir Richard Grenville of the Revenge,* London, 1937; reprinted 1949.

———*The Elizabethans and America,* London, 1959.

G. B. Parks, *Richard Hakluyt and the English Voyages,* New York, 2nd edn., 1968.

S. E. Morison, *The European Discovery of America; the Northern Voyages, A.D. 500–1600,* New York, 1971.

On the folio edition of the *Report* see:

Thomas Harriot, *A briefe and true report of the new found land of Virginia,* 1588. A facsimile edition with an introduction by R. G. Adams, Ann Arbor, 1931.

An exhaustive examination of the documents relating to the Virginia voyages, including the *Report,* is found in:

D. B. Quinn, *The Roanoke Voyages 1584-1590,* 2 vols. (Hakluyt Society), London, 1955.

The drawings of John White, with the De Bry engravings, are fully described and reproduced in facsimile in:

P. Hulton and D. B. Quinn, *The American Drawings of John White,* 2 vols., London and Chapel Hill, 1964.

A more accessible, less detailed, catalogue of the White drawings, with some reproductions in color, is contained in:

E. Croft-Murray and P. Hulton, *Catalogue of British Drawings,* [British Museum], vol. I, 2 pts., London, 1960.

On Harriot see:

H. Stevens, *Thomas Hariot,* London, 1900.

M. Rukeyser, *Traces of Thomas Hariot,* New York, 1970.

A briefe and true report
of the new found land of Virginia.
of the commodities and of the nature and man
ners of the naturall inhabitants. Discouered by
the English Colony there seated by Sir Richard
Greinuile Knight In the yeere 1585. Which Rema
zined Vnder the gouernement of twelue monethes,
At the speciall charge and direction of the Honourable SIR WALTER RALEIGH Knight lord Warden
of the stanneries Who therein hath beene fauoured
and authorised by her MAIESTIE
and her letters patents:
This fore booke Is made in English
By Thomas Hariot seruant to the abouenamed
Sir WALTER, a member of the Colony, and there.
imployed in discouering

CVM GRATIA ET PRIVILEGIO CÆS.MA^{TIS} SPECIA^{LI}

FRANCOFORTI AD MOENVM
TYPIS IOANNIS WECHELI, SVMTIBVS VERO THEODORI
DE BRY ANNO CIↃ IↃ XC.
VENALES REPERIVNTVR IN OFFICINA SIGISMVNDI FEIRABENDII

TO THE RIGHT

WORTHIE AND HONOV-
RABLE, SIR VVALTER RALEGH,

KNIGHT, SENESCHAL OF THE DVCHIES OF

Cornewall and Exeter, and L. Warden of the stannaries in Deuon
and Cornewall, T. B. wisheth true felictie.

AMORE ET VIRTVTE.

I R, seeing that the parte of the Worlde, which is betwene the
FLORIDA and the Cap BRETON nowe nammed VIRGI-
NIA, to the honneur of yours most souueraine Layde and Quee-
ne ELIZABETZ, hath ben descouuerd by yours meanes. And
great chardges. And that your Collonye hath been theer estab-
lished to your great honnor and prayse, and noe lesser proffit vnto the common

4

welth: Yt ys good raiſon that euery man eueitwe him ſelſe for to ſhowe the benè-
fit which they haue receue of yt. Theerfore, for my parte I haue been allwayes
Deſirous for to make yow knowe the good will that J haue to remayne ſtill your
moſt humble ſeruant. J haue thincke that J coldfaynde noe better occaſion to
declare yt, then takinge the paines to cott in copper (the moſt diligentye and well
that wear in my poſsible to doe) the Figures which doe leuelye repreſent the forme aud maner of the Jnhabitants of theſame countrye with theirs ceremonies,
ſollemne, feaſtes, and the manner and ſituation of their Townes, or Villages.
Addinge vnto euery figure a brief declaration of theſame, to that ende that eue-
rye man cold the better vnderſtand that which is in liuelye repreſented. Moreouer J haue thincke that the aforeſaid figures wear of greater commendation, Jf
ſomme Hiſtoire which traitinge of the commodites and fertillitye of the ſaid cou-
trye weare Ioyned with theſame, therfore haue I ſerue mi ſelfe of the rapport
which Thomas Hariot hath lattely ſett foorth, and haue cauſſe them booth togither to be printed for to dedicated vnto you, as a thiuge which by reigtte dooth
allreadye apparteyne vnto you. Therfore doe I creaue that you will accept this
little Booke, and take yt In goode partte. And deſiringe that fauor that you will
receue me in the nomber of one of your moſt humble ſeruantz, beſechinge the
lord to bleſe and further you in all yours good doinges and actions, and allſo to
preſerue, and keepe you allwayes in good helthe. And ſoe J comitt you vnto
the almyhttie, from Franckfort the firſt of Apprill 1590.

Your moſt humble ſeruant,

THEODORVS de BRY.

TO THE ADVEN-
TVRERS, FAVORERS, AND
VVELVVILLERS OF THE EN-
TERPRISE FOR THE INHABITTING
and planting in VIRGINIA.

SINCE the first vndertaking by Sir Walter Ralegh to deale in the action of difcouering of that Countrey which is now called and known by the name of VIRGINIA; many voyages hauing bin thiter made at fundrie times to his great charge; as firſt in the yeere 1584. and afterwardes in the yeeres 1585. 1586. and now of late this laſt yeare of 1587. There haue bin diuers and variable reportes with fome flaunderous and shamefull fpeeches bruited abroade by many that returned from thence. Efpecially of that difcouery which was made by the Colony tranfported by Sir Richard Greinuile in the yeare 1585. being of all the others the moſt principal and as yet of moſt effect, the time of their abode in the countrey beeing a whole yeare, when as in the other voyage before they ſtaied but fixe weekes; and the others after were onelie for fupply and tranfporation, nothing more being difcouered then had been before. Which reports haue not done a litle wrong to many that otherwife would haue alfo fauoured & aduentured in the action, to the honour and benefite of our nation, befides the particular profite and credite which would redound to them felues the dealers therein; as I hope by the fequele of euents to the shame of thofe that haue auouched the contrary shalbe manifeſt: if you the aduenturers, fauourers, and welwillers do but either encreafe in number, or in opinion continue, or hauing bin doubtfull renewe your good liking and furtherance to deale therein according to the worthineffe thereof alreadye found and as you shall vnderſtand hereafter to be requifite. Touching which woorthines through caufe of the diuerfitie of relations and reportes, manye of your opinions coulde not bee firme, nor the mindes of fome that are well difpofed, bee fetled in any certaintie.

I haue therefore thought it good beeing one that haue beene in the difcouerie and in dealing with the naturall inhabitantes fpecially imploied; and hauing therefore feene and knowne more then the ordinarie: to imparte fo much vnto you of the fruites of our labours, as that you may knowe howe iniurioufly the enterprife is flaundered. And that in publike manner at this prefent chiefelie for two refpectes.

Firſt that fome of you which are yet ignorant or doubtfull of the ſtate thereof, may fee that there is fufficiét caufe why the cheefe enterprifer with the fauour of her Maieſtie, notwithſtanding fuche reportes; hath not onelie fince continued the action by fending into the countrey againe, and replanting this laſt yeere a new Colony; but is alfo readie, according as the times and meanes will affoorde, to follow and profecute the fame.

Secondly, that you feeing and knowing the continuance of the action by the view hereof you may generally know & learne what the countrey is, & ther vpon cofider how your dealing therein if it proceede, may returne you profit and gaine; bee it either by inhabitting & planting or otherwife in furthering thereof.

And leaſt that the fubſtance of my relation should be doubtful vnto you, as of others by reafon of their diuerfitie: I will firſt open the caufe in a few wordes wherefore they are fo different; referring my felue to your fauourable conftructions, and to be adiudged of as by good confideration you shall finde caufe.

Of our companie that returned fome for their mifdemenour and ill dealing in the countrey, haue beene there worthily punished; who by reafon of their badde natures, haue malicioufly not onelie fpoken ill of their Gouernours; but for their fakes flaundered the countrie it felfe. The like alfo haue thofe done which were of their confort.

Some beeing ignorant of the ftate thereof, notwithftanding fince their returne amogeft their friendes and acquaintance and alfo others, efpecially if they were in compaine where they might not be gainefaide; woulde feeme to knowe fo much as no men more; and make no men fo great trauailers as themfelues. They ftood fo much as it maie feeme vppon their credite and reputation that hauing been a twelue moneth in the countrey, it woulde haue beene a great difgrace vnto them as they thought, if they coulde not haue faide much wheter it were true or falfe. Of which fome haue fpoken of more then euer they faw or otherwife knew to bee there; otherfome haue not bin ashamed to make abfolute deniall of that which although not by thē, yet by others is moft certainely ād there plētifully knowne. And otherfome make difficulties of thofe things they haue no skill of.

The caufe of their ignorance was, in that they were of that many that were neuer out of the Iland where wee were feated, or not farre, or at the leaftwife in few places els, during the time of our aboade in the countrey; or of that many that after golde and filuer was not fo foone found, as it was by them looked for, had little or no care of any other thing but to pamper their bellies; or of that many which had little vnderftanding, leffe difcretion, and more tongue then was needfull or requifite.

Some alfo were of a nice bringing vp, only in cities or townes, or fuch as neuer (as I may fay) had feene the world before. Becaufe there were not to bee found any English cities, nor fuch faire houfes, nor at their owne wish any of their olde accuftomed daintie food, nor any foft beds of downe or fethers: the countrey was to them miferable, & their reports thereof according.

Becaufe my purpofe was but in briefe to open the caufe of the varietie of fuch fpeeches; the particularities of them, and of many enuious, malicious, and flaūderous reports and deuifes els, by our owne countrey men befides; as trifles that are not worthy of wife men to bee thought vpon, I meane not to trouble you withall: but will paffe to the commodities, the fubftance of that which I haue to make relation of vnto you.

The treatife where of for your more readie view & eafier vnderftanding I will diuide into three fpeciall parts. In the firft I will make declaration of fuch commodities there alreadie found or to be raifed, which will not onely ferue the ordinary turnes of you which are and shall bee the plāters and inhabitants, but fuch an ouerplus fufficiently to bee yelded, or by men of skill to bee prouided, as by way of trafficke and exchaunge with our owne nation of England, will enrich your felues the prouiders; thofe that shal deal with you; the enterprifers in general; and greatly profit our owne countrey men, to fupply them with moft things which heretofore they haue bene faine to prouide, either of ftrangers or of our enemies: which commodities for diftinction fake, I call *Merchantable.*

In the fecond, I will fet downe all the cōmodities which wee know the countrey by our experience doeth yeld of it felfe for victuall, and fuftenance of mans life; fuch as is vfually fed vpon by the inhabitants of the countrey, as alfo by vs during the time we were there.

In the laft part I will make mention generally of fuch other cōmodities befides, as I am able to remember, and as I shall thinke behoofull for thofe that shall inhabite, and plant there to knowe of; which fpecially concerne building, as alfo fome other neceffary vfes: with a briefe defcription of the nature and maners of the people of the countrey.

THE FIRST PART,
OF MARCHAN-
TABLE COMMO-
DITIES.

Silke of graſſe or graſſe Silke.

Here is a kind of graſſe in the countrey vppon the blades where of there groweth very good ſilke in forme of a thin glittering skin to bee ſtript of. It groweth two foote and a halfe high or better: the blades are about two foot in length, and half inch broad. The like groweth in Perſia, which is in the ſelfe ſame climate as Virginia, of which very many of the ſilke workes that come from thence into Europe are made. Here of if it be planted and ordered as in Perſia, it cannot in reaſon be otherwiſe, but that there will riſe in ſhorte time great profite to the dealers therein; ſeeing there is ſo great vſe and vent thereof as well in our countrey as els where. And by the meanes of ſowing & plāting in good ground, it will be farre greater, better, and more plentifull then it is. Although notwithſtanding there is great ſtore thereof in many places of the countrey growing naturally and wilde. Which alſo by proofe here in England, in making a piece of ſilke Grogran, we found to be excellent good.

Worme Silke.

In manie of our iourneyes we found ſilke wormes fayre and great; as bigge as our ordinary walnuttes. Although it hath not beene our happe to haue found ſuch plentie as elſew here to be in the coutrey we haue heard of; yet ſeeing that the countrey doth naturally breede and nouriſh them, there is no doubt but if art be added in plantig of mulbery trees and others fitte for them in commodious places, for their feeding and nourishing; and some of them carefully gathered and husbanded in that sort as by men of skill is knowne to be necessarie: there will rise as great profite in time to the Virginians, as there of doth now to the Persians, Turkes, Italians and Spaniards.

Flaxe and Hempe.

The trueth is that of Hempe and Flaxe there is no great store in any one place together, by reason it is not planted but as the soile doth yeeld it of it selfe; and howsoeuer the leafe, and stemme or stalke doe differ from ours; the stuffe by the iudgemēt of men of skill is altogether as good as ours. And if not, as further proofe should finde otherwise; we haue that experience of the soile, as thas there canno bee shewed anie reason to the contrary, but that it will grow there excellent well; and by planting will be yeelded plentifully: seeing there is so much ground whereof some may well be applyed to such purposes. What benefite heereof may growe in cordage and linnens who can not easily vnderstand?

Allum.

There is a veine of earth along the sea coast for the space of fourtie or fiftie miles, whereof by the iudgement of some that haue made triall heere in England, is made good Allum, of that kinde which is called Roche Allum. The richnesse of such a commoditie is so well knowne that I neede not to saye any thing thereof. The same earth doth also yeelde White Copresse, Nitrum, and Alumen Plumeum, but nothing so plentifully as the common Allum; which be also of price and profitable.

Wapeih:

Wapeih, a kinde of earth so called by the naturall inhabitants; very like to terra sigillata: and hauing beene refined, it hath beene found by some of our Phisitiōs and Chirurgeons to bee of the same kinde of vertue and more effectuall. The inhabitāts vse it very much for the cure of sores and woundes: there is in diuers places great plentie, and in some places of a blewe sort.

Pitch, Tarre, Rozen, and Turpentine.

There are those kindes of trees which yeelde them abundantly and great store. In the very same Iland where wee were seated, being fifteene miles of length, and fiue or sixe miles in breadth, there are fewe trees els but of the same kind; the whole Iland being full.

Sassafras.

Saffafras.

Saffafras, called by the inhabitantes *Winauk*, a kinde of wood of moft pleafand and fweete fmel; and of moft rare vertues in phifick for the cure of many difeafes. It is found by experience to bee farre better and of more vfes then the wood which is called *Guaiacum*, or *Lignum vitæ*. For the defcription, the manner of vfing and the manifolde vertues thereof, I referre you to the booke of *Monardus*, tranflated and entituled in English, *The ioyfull newes from the Weft Indies*.

Cedar.

Cedar, a very fweet wood & fine timber; wherof if nefts of chefts be there made, or timber therof fitted for fweet & fine bedfteads, tables, deskes, lutes, virginalles & many things elfe, (of which there hath beene proofe made already) to make vp fraite with other principal commodities will yeeld profite.

Wine.

There are two kinds of grapes that the foile doth yeeld naturally : the one is fmall and fowre of the ordinarie bigneffe as ours in England: the other farre greater & of himfelfe iushious fweet. When they are pläted and hufbandeg as they ought, a principall commoditie of wines by them may be raifed.

Oyle.

There are two fortes of *Walnuttes* both holding oyle, but the one farre more plentifull then the other. When there are milles & other deuifes for the purpofe, a commodity of them may be raifed becaufe there are infinite ftore. There are alfo three feuerall kindes of *Berries* in the forme of Oke akornes, which alfo by the experience and vfe of the inhabitantes, wee finde to yeelde very good and fweete oyle. Furthermore the *Beares* of the countrey are commonly very fatte, and in fome places there are many: their fatneffe becaufe it is fo liquid, may well be termed oyle, and hath many fpeciall vfes.

Furres:

All along the Sea coaft there are great ftore of *Otters*, which beeyng taken by weares and other engines made for the purpofe, will yeelde good profite. Wee hope alfo of *Marterne furres*, and make no doubt by the relation of the people but that in fome places of the countrey there are ftore: although there were but two skinnes that came to our handes. *Luzarnes* alfo we haue vnderftäding of, although for the time we faw none.

Deare skinnes.

Deare skinnes dreſſed after the manner of *Chamoes* or vndreſſed are to be had of the naturall inhabitants thouſands yeerely by way of trafficke for trifles : and no more waſt or ſpoile of Deare then is and hath beene ordinarily in time before.

Ciuet cattes.

In our trauailes, there was founde one to haue beene killed by a ſaluage or in-habitant: and in an other place the ſmell where one or more had lately beene befo-re: whereby we gather beſides then by the relation of the people that there are ſo-me in the countrey: good profite will riſe by them.

Iron.

In two places of the countrey ſpecially, one about foureſcore and the other ſixe ſcore miles from the Fort or place where wee dwelt : wee founde neere the wa-ter ſide the ground to be rockie, which by the triall of a minerall man, was founde to holde Iron richly. It is founde in manie places of the countrey elſe. I knowe no-thing to the contrarie, but that it maie bee allowed for a good marchantable com-moditie, conſidering there the ſmall charge for the labour and feeding of men : the infinite ſtore of wood: the want of wood and deereneſſe thereof in England: & the neceſſity of ballaſting of ſhippes.

Copper.

A hundred and fiftie miles into the maine in two townes wee founde with the inhabitaunts diuerſe ſmall plates of copper , that had beene made as wee vnder-ſtood, by the inhabitantes that dwell farther into the countrey : where as they ſay are mountaines and Riuers that yeelde alſo whyte graynes of Mettall, which is to bee deemed *Siluer*. For confirmation whereof at the time of our firſt arriuall in the Countrey, I ſawe with ſome others with mee , two ſmall peeces of ſiluer groſly bea-ten about the weight of a Teſtrone, hangyng in the eares of a *Wiroans* or *chiefe Lorde* that dwelt about foureſcore myles from vs ; of whom thorowe enquiry , by the number of dayes and the way , I learned that it had come to his handes from the ſame place or neere, where I after vnderſtood the copper was made and the whi-te graynes of mettall founde. The aforeſaide copper wee alſo founde by triall to holde ſiluer.

Pearle.

Sometimes in feeding on muſcles wee founde ſome pearle; but it was our hap to meete with ragges, or of a pide colour; not hauing yet diſcouered thoſe

places

places where wee hearde of better and more plentie. One of our companie; a man of skill in ſuch matters, had gathered together from among the ſauage people a-boute fiue thouſande: of which number he choſe ſo many as made a fayre chaine, which for their likeneſſe and vniformitie in roundneſſe, orientneſſe, and pideneſſe of mãny excellent colours, with equalitie in greatneſſe, were verie fayre and rare; and had therefore beene preſented to her Maieſtie, had wee not by caſualtie and trough extremity of a ſtorme, loſt them with many things els in comming away from the countrey.

Sweete Gummes.

Sweete Gummes of diuers kindes and many other Apothecary drugges of which wee will make ſpeciall mention, when wee ſhall receiue it from ſuch men of skill in that kynd, that in taking reaſonable paines ſhall diſcouer them more parti-cularly then wee haue done; and than now I can make relation of, for want of the examples I had prouited and gathered, and are nowe loſt, with other thinges by caſualtie before mentioned.

Dyes of diuers kindes.

There is Shoemake well knowen, and vſed in England for blacke; the ſeede of an hearbe called Waſewówr: little ſmall rootes called Cháppacor; and the barke of the tree called by the inhabitaunts Tangomóckonomindge: which Dies are for diuers ſortes of red: their goodneſſe for our Engliſh clothes remayne yet to be pro-ued. The inhabitants vſe them onely for the dying of hayre; and colouring of their faces, aud Mantles made of Deare skinnes; and alſo for the dying of Ruſhes to ma-ke artificiall workes withall in their Mattes and Baskettes; hauing no other thing beſides that they account of, apt to vſe them for. If they will not proue merchan-table there is no doubt but the Planters there ſhall finde apte vſes for them, as alſo for other colours which wee knowe to be there.

Oade.

A thing of ſo great vent and vſe amongſt Engliſh Diers, which cannot bee yeelded ſufficiently in our owne countrey for ſpare of ground; may bee planted in Virginia, there being ground enough. The grouth therof need not to be doubted when as in the Ilandes of the Aſores it groweth plentifully, which is in theſame cli-mate. So likewiſe of Madder.

Suger canes.

Whe carried thither Suger canes to plant which beeing not ſo well preſerued as was requiſit, & beſides the time of the yere being paſt for their ſetting when we arriued, wee could not make that proofe of them as wee defired. Notwithſtã ding ſeeing that they grow in the ſame climate, in the South part of Spaine and in Bar-bary, our hope in reaſon may yet continue. So likewiſe for *Orenges*, and *Lemmons*, there may be planted alſo *Quinſes*. Wherbi may grow in reaſonable time if the a-ction be diligently proſecuted, no ſmall commodities in *Sugers*, *Suckets*, and *Mar-malades*.

Many other commodities by planting may there alſo bee raiſed, which I lea-ue to your diſcret and gentle conſiderations: and many alſo may bee there which yet we haue not diſcouered. Two more commodities of great value one of certain-tie, and the other in hope, not to be planted, but there to be raiſed & in ſhort time to be prouided and prepared, I might haue ſpecified. So likewiſe of thoſe commo-dities already ſet downe I might haue ſaid more; as of the particular places where they are founde and beſt to be planted and prepared: by what meanes and in what reaſonable ſpace of time they might be raiſed to profit and in what proportion; but becauſe others then welwillers might bee therewithall acquainted, not to the good of the action, I haue wittingly omitted them: knowing that to thoſe that are well diſpoſed I haue vttered, according to my promiſe and purpoſe, for this part ſuffi-cient.

THE

THE SECOND PART,
OF SVCHE COMMO-
DITIES AS VIRGINIA IS
knowne to yeelde for victuall and suftenáce of mans
life, vfually fed vpon by the naturall inhabitants:
as alfo by vs during the time of our aboad.
And firft of fuch as are fowed
and husbanded.

PAGATOWR, a kinde of graine fo called by the inhabitants; the
fame in the Weft Indies is called MAYZE: Englifh men call it
Guinney wheate or Turkie wheate, according to the names of the
countreys from whence the like hath beene brought. The graine
is about the bigneffe of our ordinary Englifh peaze and not much
different in forme and fhape: but of diuers colours: fome white,
fome red, fome yellow, and fome blew. All of them yeelde a very white and fweete
flowre: beeing vfed according to his kinde it maketh a very good bread. Wee made
of the fame in the countrey fome mault, whereof was brued as good ale as was to
bee defired. So likewife by the help of hops therof may bee made as good Beere. It
is a graine of marucilous great increafe; of a thoufand, fifteene hundred and fome
two thoufand fold. There are three fortes, of which two are ripe in an eleuen and
twelue weekes at the moft: fometimes in ten, after the time they are fet, and are
then of height in ftalke about fixe or feuen foote. The other fort is ripe in fourtee-
ne, and is about ten foote high, of the ftalkes fome beare foure heads, fome three,
fome one, and two: euery head cötaining fiue, fixe, or feuë hundred graines within
a fewe more or leffe. Of thefe graines befides bread, the inhabitants make victuall

eyther by parching them; or feething them whole vntill they be broken; or boyling the floure with water into a pappe.

Okindgier, called by vs *Beanes*, becaufe in greatneffe & partly in fhape they are like to the Beanes in England; fauing that they are flatter, of more diuers colours, and fome pide. The leafe alfo of the ftemme is much different. In tafte they are altogether as good as our Englifh peaze.

Wickonzówr, called by vs *Peaze*, in refpect of the beanes for diftinction fake, becaufe they are much leffe; although in forme they little differ; but in goodneffe of taft much, & are far better then our English peaze. Both the beanes and peaze are ripe in tenne weekes after they are fet. They make them victuall either by boyling them all to pieces into a broth; or boiling them whole vntill they bee foft and beginne to breake as is vfed in England, eyther by themfelues or mixtly together: Sometime they mingle of the wheate with them. Sometime alfo beeing whole fodden, they brufe or pound them in a morter, & thereof make loaues or lumps of dowifhe bread, which they vfe to eat for varietie.

Macócqwer, according to their feuerall formes called by vs, *Pompions*, *Mellions*, and *Gourdes*, becaufe they are of the like formes as thofe kindes in England. In *Virginia* fuch of feuerall formes are of one tafte and very good, and do alfo fpring from one feed. There are of two forts; one is ripe in the fpace of a moneth, and the other in two moneths.

There is an hearbe which in Dutch is called *Melden*. Some of thofe that I defcribe it vnto, take it to be a kinde of Orage; it groweth about foure or fiue foote high: of the feede thereof they make a thicke broth, and pottage of a very good tafte: of the ftalke by burning into afhes they make a kinde of falt earth, wherewithall many vfe fometimes to feafon their brothes; other falte they knowe not. Wee our felues, vfed the leaues alfo for pothearbes.

There is alfo another great hearbe in forme of a Marigolde, ahout fixe foote in height; the head with the floure is a fpanne in breadth. Some take it to bee *Planta Solis*: of the feedes heereof they make both a kinde of bread and broth.

All the aforefaide commodities for victuall are fet or fowed, fometimes in groundes a part and feuerally by themfelues; but for the moft part together in one ground mixtly: the manner thereof with the dreffing and preparing of the groũd, becaufe I will note vnto you the fertilitie of the foile; I thinke good briefly to defcribe.

The ground they neuer fatten with mucke, dounge or any other thing; neither plow nor digge it as we in England, but onely prepare it in fort as followeth. A fewe daies before they fowe or fet, the men with wooden inftruments, made almoft in forme of mattockes or hoes with long handles; the women with fhort peckers or parers, becaufe they vfe them fitting, of a foote long and about fiue inches in breadth: doe onely breake the vpper part of the ground to rayfe vp the weedes, graffe, & old ftubbes of corne ftalkes with their rootes. The which after a day or twoes

drying

drying in the Sunne, being fcrapte vp into many fmall heapes, to faue them labour for carrying them away ; they burne into afhes. (And whereas fome may thinke that they vfe the afhes for to better the grounde; I fay that then they woulde eyther difperfe the afhes abroade; which wee obferued they doe not, except the heapes bee too great: or els would take fpeciall care to fet their corne where the afhes lie, which alfo wee finde they are careleffe of.) And this is all the hufbanding of their ground that they vfe.

Then their fetting or fowing is after this maner. Firft for their corne, beginning in one corner of the plot, with a pecker they make a hole, wherein they put foure graines with that care they touch not one another, (about an inch afunder) and couer them with the moulde againe : and fo through out the whole plot, making fuch holes and vfing them after fuch maner: but with this regard that they bee made in rankes, euery rake differing from other halfe a fadome or a yarde, and the holes alfo in euery ranke, as much. By this meanes there is a yarde fpare ground betwene euery hole: where according to difcretion here and there, they fet as many Beanes and Peaze: in diuers places alfo among the feedes of *Macócqwer, Melden* and *Planta Solis.*

The ground being thus fet according to the rate by vs experimented, an English Acre conteining fourtie pearches in length, and foure in breadth, doeth there yeeld in croppe or ofcome of corne, beanes, and peaze, at the leaft two hūdred London bufhelles: befides the *Macócqwer, Melden,* and *Planta Solis* : When as in England fourtie bufhelles of our wheate yeelded out of fuch an acre is thought to be much.

I thought alfo good to note this vnto you, if you which fhall inhabite and plant there, maie know how fpecially that countrey corne is there to be preferred before ours : Befides the manifold waies in applying it to victuall, the increafe is fo much that fmall labour and paines is needful in refpect that muft be vfed for ours. For this I can affure you that according to the rate we haue made proofe of, one man may prepare and hufbane fo much grounde (hauing once borne corne before) with leffe thē foure and twentie houres labour, as fhall yeelde him victuall in a large proportiō for a twelue mōeth, if hee haue nothing elfe, but that which the fame groūd will yeelde, and of that kinde onelie which I haue before fpoken of: the faide groūd being alfo but of fiue and twentie yards fquare. And if neede require, but that there is ground enough, there might be raifed out of one and the felffame ground two harueftes or ofcomes; for they fowe or fet and may at anie time when they thinke good from the middeft of March vntill the ende of Iune: fo that they alfo fet when they haue eaten of their firft croppe. In fome places of the countrey notwithftanding they haue two haruefts, as we haue heard, out of one and the fame ground.

For Englifh corne neuerthelefe whether to vfe or not to vfe it, you that inhabite maie do as you fhall haue farther caufe to thinke beft. Of the grouth you need not to doubt: for barlie, oates and peaze, we haue feene proof of, not beeing purpofely

ſowen but fallen caſually in the worſt ſort of ground, and yet to be as faire as any we
haue euer ſeene here in England. But of wheat becauſe it was muſty and hat taken
ſalt water wee could make no triall : and of rye we had none. Thus much haue I di-
greſſed and I hope not vnneceſſarily: nowe will I returne againe to my courſe and
intreate of that which yet remaineth appertaining to this Chapter.

There is an herbe which is ſowed a part by it ſelfe & is called by the inhabitants
Vppówoc: In the Weſt Indies it hath diuers names, according to the ſeuerall places
& countries where it groweth and is vſed : The Spaniardes generally call it Tobacco. The leaues thereof being dried and brought into powder: they vſe to take the
fume or ſmoke thereof by ſucking it through pipes made of claie into their ſtoma-
cke and heade; from whence it purgeth ſuperfluous fleame & other groſſe humors,
openeth all the pores & paſſages of the body: by which meanes the vſe thereof, not
only preſerueth the body from obſtructiós; but alſo if any be, ſo that they haue not
beene of too long continuance, in ſhort time breaketh them: wherby their bodies
are notably preſerued in health, & know not many greeuous diſeaſes wherewithall
wee in England are oftentimes afflicted.

This Vppówoc is of ſo precious eſtimation amongeſt then, that they thinke
their gods are marueloufly delighted therwith : Wherupon ſometime they make
hallowed fires & caſt ſome of the pouder therein for a ſacrifice : being in a ſtorme
vppon the waters, to pacifie their gods , they caſt ſome vp into the aire and into the
water: ſo a weare for fiſh being newly ſet vp, they caſt ſome therein and into the aire: alſo after an eſcape of danger, they caſt ſome into the aire likewiſe : but all done
with ſtrange geſtures, ſtamping, ſomtime dauncing, clapping of hands, holding vp
of hands, & ſtaring vp into rhe heauens, vttering therewithal and chattering ſtrange words & noiſes.

We our ſelues during the time we were there vſed to ſuck it after their maner,
as alſo ſince our returne, & haue found maine rare and wonderful experiments of
the vertues thereof; of which the relation woulde require a volume by it ſelfe : the
vſe of it by ſo manie of late, men & women of great calling as elſe, and ſome learned
Phiſitions alſo, is ſufficient witnes.

And theſe are all the commodities for ſuſtenance of life that I know and can
remember they vſe to huſband: all elſe that followe are founde growing naturally
or wilde.

Of Rootes.

OPENAVK are a kind of roots of round forme , ſome of the bignes of walnuts, ſome far greater, which are found in moiſt & mariſh grounds growing many
together one by another in ropes, or as thogh they were faſtnened with a ſtring.
Being boiled or ſodden they are very good meate.

OKEEPENAVK are alſo of round ſhape, found in dry grounds : ſome are
of the

of the bignes of a mans head.   They are to be eaten as they are taken out of the ground, for by reafon of their drineffe they will neither rofte nor feeth.   Their taft is not fo good as of the former rootes, notwithstanding for want of bread & fomtimes for varietie the inhabitants vfe to eate them with fish or flesh, and in my iudgement they doe as well as the houshold bread made of rie heere in England.

Kaishúcpenauk a white kind of roots about the bignes of hen egs & nere of that forme: their taft was not fo good to our feeming as of the other, and therfore their place and manner of growing not fo much cared for by vs: the inhabitāts notwithstanding vfed to boile & eate many.

Tfinaw a kind of roote much like vnto the which in England is called the *China root* brought from the Eaft Indies. And we know not anie thing to the cōtrary but that it maie be of the fame kind. Thefe roots grow manie together in great clufters and doe bring foorth a brier ftalke, but the leafe in shape far vnlike; which beeing fupported by the trees it groweth neereft vnto, wil reach or climbe to the top of the higheft. From thefe roots while they be new or fresh beeing chopt into fmall pieces & ftampt, is ftrained with water a iuice that maketh bread, & alfo being boiled, a very good fpoonemeate in maner of a gelly, and is much better in taft if it bee tempered with oyle. This *Tfinaw* is not of that fort which by fome was caufed to be brought into England for the *China roote*, for it was difcouered fince, and is in vfe as is afore faide: but that which was brought hither is not yet knowne neither by vs nor by the inhabitants to ferue for any vfe or purpofe; although the rootes in shape are very like.

Cofcúshaw, fome of our company tooke to bee that kinde of roote which the Spaniards in the Weft Indies call *Caffauy*, whereupon alfo many called it by that name: it groweth in very muddie pooles and moift groundes. Being dreffed according to the countrey maner, it maketh a good bread, and alfo a good fponemeate, and is vfed very much by the inhabitants: The iuice of this root is poifon, and therefore heede muft be taken before any thing be made therewithal: Either the rootes muft bee firft fliced and dried in the Sunne, or by the fire, and then being pounded into floure wil make good bread: or els while they are greene they are to bee pared, cut into pieces and ftampt; loues of the fame to be laid neere or ouer the fire vntill it be foure, and then being well pounded againe, bread, or fpone meate very good in tafte, and holfome may be made thereof.

Habafcon is a roote of hoat tafte almoft of the forme and bigneffe of a Parfeneepe, of it felfe it is no victuall, but onely a helpe beeing boiled together with other meates.

There are alfo *Leekes* differing little from ours in England that grow in many places of the countrey, of which, when we came in places where, wee gathered and eate many, but the naturall inhabitants neuer.

Of Fruites.

CHESTNVTS, there are in diuers places great store: some they vse to eate rawe, some they stampe and boile to make spoonemeate, and with some being sodden they make such a manner of dowe bread as they vse of their beanes before mentioned.

WALNVTS: There are two kindes of Walnuts, and of then infinit store: In many places where very great woods for many miles together the third part of trees are walnuttrees. The one kind is of the same taste and forme or litle differing from ours of England , but that they are harder and thicker shelled: the other is greater and hath a verie ragged and harde shell : but the kernell great, verie oylie and sweete. Besides their eating of them after our ordinarie maner, they breake them with stones and pound them in morters with water to make a milk which they vse to put into some sorts of their spoonmeate; also among their sodde wheat, peaze, beanes and pompions which maketh them haue a farre more pleasant taste.

MEDLARS a kind of verie good fruit, so called by vs chieflie for these respectes : first in that they are not good vntill they be rotten : then in that they open at the head as our medlars, and are about the same bignesse: otherwise in taste and colour they are farre differēt : for they are as red as cheries and very sweet: but whereas the cherie is sharpe sweet, they are lushious sweet.

METAQVESVNNAVK, a kinde of pleasaunt fruite almost of the shape & bignes of English peares, but that they are of a perfect red colour as well within as without. They grow on a plant whose leaues are verie thicke and full of prickles as sharpe as needles. Some that haue bin in the Indies, where they haue seen that kind of red die of great price which is called Cochinile to grow , doe describe his plant right like vnto this of Metaquesunnauk but whether it be the true Cochinile or a bastard or wilde kind, it cannot yet be certified; seeing that also as I heard, Cochinile is not of the fruite but founde on the leaues of the plant ; which leaues for such matter we haue not so specially obserued.

GRAPES there are of two sorts which I mentioned in the marchantable cōmodities.

STRABERIES there are as good & as great as those which we haue in our English gardens.

MVLBERIES, Applecrabs, Hurts or Hurtleberies , such as wee haue in England.

SACQVENVMMENER a kinde of berries almost like vnto capres but somewhat greater which grow together in clusters vpon a plant or herb that is found in shalow waters: being boiled eight or nine hours according to their kind are very good meate and holesome, otherwise if they be eaten they will make a man for the time franticke or extremely sicke.

There is a kind of reed which beareth a seed almost like vnto our rie or wheat, & being boiled is good meate.

In

In our trauailes in some places wee founde *wilde peaze* like vnto ours in England but that they were lesse, which are also good meate.

Of a kinde of fruite or berrie in forme of Acornes.

There is a kind of berrie or acorne, of which there are fiue sorts that grow on seuerall kinds of trees; the one is called *Sagatémener*, the second *Osamener*, the third *Pummuckóner*. These kind of acorns they vse to drie vpon hurdles made of reeds with fire vnderneath almost after the maner as we dry malt in England. When they are to be vsed they first water them vntil they be soft & then being sod they make a good victuall, either to eate so simply, or els being also pounded, to make loaues or lumpes of bread. These be also the three kinds of which, I said before, the inhabitants vsed to make sweet oyle.

An other sort is called *Sapúmmener* which being boiled or parched doth eate and taste like vnto chestnuts. They sometime also make bread of this sort.

The fifth sort is called *Mangúmmenauk*, and is the acorne of their kind of oake, the which beeing dried after the maner of the first sortes, and afterward watered they boile them, & their seruants or sometime the chiefe themselues either for variety or for want of bread, doe eate them with their fish or flesh.

Of Beastes.

Deare, in some places there are great store: neere vnto the sea coast they are of the ordinarie bignes as ours in England, & some lesse: but further vp into the countrey where there is better feed they are greater: they differ from ours onely in this, their tailes are longer and the snags of their hornes looke backward.

Conies, Those that we haue seen & al that we can heare of are of a grey colour like vnto hares: in some places there are such pletie that all the people of some townes make them mantles of the furre or flue of the skinnes of those they vsually take.

Saquenúckot & Maquówoc; two kindes of small beastes greater then conies which are very good meat. We neuer tooke any of them our selues, but sometime eate of such as the inhabitants had taken & brought vnto vs.

Squirels which are of a grey colour, we haue taken & eaten.

Beares which are all of black colour. The beares of this countrey are good meat; the inhabitants in time of winter do vse to take & eate manie, so also somtime did wee. They are taken comonlie in this sort. In some Ilands or places where they are, being hunted for, as soone as they haue spiall of a man they presently run awaie, & then being chased they clime and get vp the next tree they can, from whence with arrowes they are shot downe starke dead, or with those wounds that they may after easily bekilled; we sometime shotte them downe with our caleeuers.

I haue the names of eight & twenty seuerall sortes of beasts which I haue heard of to be here and there dispersed in the countrie, especially in the maine: of which there are only twelue kinds that we haue yet discouered, & of those that be good meat we know only them before mentioned. The inhabitânts somtime kil the *Lyon* & eat him: & we somtime as they came to our hands of their *Wolues* or *woluish Dogges*, which I haue not set downe for good meat, least that some woulde vnderstand my iudgement therin to be more simple than needeth, although I could alleage the difference in taste of those kindes from ours, which by some of our company haue beene experimented in both.

Of Foule.

Turkie cockes and *Turkie hennes*: *Stockdoues*: *Partridges*: *Cranes*: *Hernes*: & in winter great store of *Swannes* & *Geese*. Of al sortes of foule I haue the names in the countrie language of four escore and sixe of which number besides those that be named, we haue taken, eaten, & haue the pictures as they were there drawne with the names of the inhabitaunts of seuerall strange sortes of water foule eight, and seuenteene kinds more of land foul, although wee haue seen and eaten of many more, which for want of leasure there for the purpose coulde not bee pictured: and after wee are better furnished and stored vpon further discouety, with their strange beastes, fishe, trees, plants, and hearbes, they shall bee also published.

There are also *Parats, Faulcons, & Marlin haukes*, which although with vs they bee not vsed for meate, yet for other causes I thought good to mention.

Of Fishe.

For foure monethes of the yeere, February, March, Aprill and May, there are plentie of *Sturgeons*: And also in the same monethes of *Herrings*, some of the ordinary bignesse as ours in England, but the most part farre greater, of eighteene, twentie inches, and some two foote in length and better; both these kindes of fishe in those monethes are most plentifull, and in best season, which wee founde to bee most delicate and pleasaunt meate.

There are also *Troutes, Porpoises, Rayes, Oldwiues, Mullets, Plaice*, and very many other sortes of excellent good fish, which we haue taken & eaten, whose names I know not but in the countrey language; wee haue of twelue sorts more the pictures as they were drawn in the countrey with their names.

The inhabitants vse to take then two maner of wayes, the one is by a kind of wear made of reedes which in that countrey are very strong. The other way which is more strange, is with poles made sharpe at one ende, by shooting them into the fish after the maner as Irishmen cast dartes; either as they are rowing in their boates or els as they are wading in the shallowes for the purpose.

There

There are alſo in many places plentie of theſe kindes which follow.

Sea crabbes, ſuch as we haue in England.

Oyſtres, ſome very great, and ſome ſmall; ſome rounde and ſome of a long ſhape : They are founde both in ſalt water and brackiſh, and thoſe that we had out of ſalt water are far better than the other as in our owne countrey.

Alſo *Muſcles, Scalopes, Periwinkles,* and *Creuiſes.*

Seekanauk, a kinde of cruſtie shell fiſhe which is good meate, about a foote in breadth, hauing a cruſtie tayle, many legges like a crab ; and her eyes in her backe. They are founde in shallowes of ſalt waters; and ſometime on the shoare.

There are many *Tortoyſes* both of lande and ſea kinde, their backes & bellies are shelled very thicke ; their head, feete, and taile, which are in appearance, ſeeme ougly as though they were membres of a ſerpent or venemous : but notwithſtanding they are very good meate, as alſo their egges. Some haue bene founde of a yard in bredth and better.

And thus haue I made relation of all ſortes of victuall that we fed vpon for the time we were in *Virginia,* as alſo the inhabitants themſelues, as farre foorth as I knowe and can remember or that are ſpecially worthy to bee re-membred.

THE THIRD AND
LAST PART,
OF SVCH OTHER
THINGES AS IS BE HOO-
full for thofe which shall plant and inhabit to
know of; with a defcription of the nature
and manners of the people of
the countrey.

*Of commodities for building and other
neceſſary vſes.*

Hofe other things which I am more to make rehear-
fall of, are fuch as concerne building, and other mecha-
nicall neceſſarie vſes; as diuers fortes of trees for houfe
& ship timber, and other vſes els: Alfo lime, ftone, and
brick, leaft that being not mentioned fome might haue bene doubted of, or by fome that are malicious re-
ported the contrary.

 Okes, there are as faire, ftraight, tall, and as good
timber as any can be, and alfo great ftore, and in fome
places very great.

 W*alnut trees*, as I haue faide before very many, fome haue bene feen excellent
faire timber of foure & fiue fadome, & aboue fourefcore foot ftreight without
bough.

 Firre trees fit for mafts of ships, fome very tall & great.

Rakiock,

Rakíock, a kind of trees so called that are sweet wood of which the inhabitans that were neere vnto vs doe commonly make their boats or Canoes of the form of trowes; only with the helpe of fire, harchets of stones, and shels; we haue known some so great being made in that sort of one tree that they haue carried well xx. men at once, besides much baggage: the timber being great, tal, streight, soft, light, & yet tough enough I thinke (besides other vses) to be fit also for masts of ships.

Cedar, a sweet wood good for seelings, Chests, Boxes, Bedsteedes, Lutes, Virginals, and many things els, as I haue also said before. Some of our company which haue wandered in some places where I haue not bene, haue made certaine affirmation of *Cyprus* which for such and other excellent vses, is also a wood of price and no small estimation.

Maple, and also *Wich-hazle*, wherof the inhabitants vse to make their bowes.

Holly a necessary thing for the making of birdlime.

Willowes good for the making of weares and weeles to take fish after the English manner, although the inhabitants vse only reedes, which becaufe they are so strong as also flexible, do serue for that turne very well and sufficiently.

Beech and *Ashe*, good for caske, hoopes: and if neede require, plow worke, as also for many things els.

Elme.

Sassafras trees.

Ascopo a kinde of tree very like vnto Lawrell, the barke is hoat in tast and spicie, it is very like to that tree which Monardus describeth to bee *Cassia Lignea* of the West Indies.

There are many other strange trees whose names I knowe not but in the *Virginian* language, of which I am not nowe able, neither is it so conuenient for the present to trouble you with particular relatió: seeing that for timber and other necessary vses I haue named sufficient: And of many of the rest but that they may be applied to good vse, I know no cause to doubt.

Now for Stone, Bricke and Lime, thus it is. Neere vnto the Sea coast where wee dwelt, there are no kinde of stones to bee found (except a fewe small pebbles about foure miles off) but such as haue bene brought from farther out of the maine. In some of our voiages wee haue seene diuers hard raggie stones, great pebbles, and a kinde of grey stone like vnto marble, of which the inhabitants make their hatchets to cleeue wood. Vpon inquirie wee heard that a little further vp into the Countrey were of all sortes verie many, although of Quarries they are ignorant, neither haue they vse of any store whereupon they should haue occasion to seeke any. For if euerie housholde haue one or two to cracke Nuttes, grinde shelles, whet copper, and sometimes other stones for hatchets, they haue enough: neither vse they any digging, but onely for graues about three foote deepe: and therefore no maruaile that they know neither Quarries, nor lime stones, which both may bee in places neerer than they wot of.

In the meane time vntill there bee difcouerie of fufficient ftore in fome place or other cóuenient, the want of you which are and shalbe the planters therein may be as well fupplied by Bricke : for the making whereof in diuers places of the countrey there is clay both excellent good, and plentie ; and alfo by lime made of Oifter shels, and of others burnt, after the maner as they vfe in the Iles of Tenct and Shepy, and alfo in diuers other places of England: Which kinde of lime is well knowne to bee as good as any other. And of Oifter shels there is plentie enough: for befides diuers other particular places where are abundance, there is one shallowe founde along the coaft, where for the fpace of many miles together in lenght, and two or three miles in breadth, the grounde is nothing els beeing but halfe a foote or a foote vnder water for the moft part.

This much can I fay further more of ftones, that about 120. miles from our fort neere the water in the fide of a hill was founde by a Gentleman of our company, a great veine of hard ragge ftones, which I thought good to remember vnto you.

Of the nature and manners of the people

It refteth I fpeake a word or two of the naturall inhabitants, their natures and maners, leauing large difcourfe thereof vntill time more conuenient hereafter : nowe onely fo farre foorth, as that you may know, how that they in refpect of troubling our inhabiting and planting, are not to be feared; but that they shall haue caufe both to feare and loue vs, that shall inhabite with them.

They are a people clothed with loofe mantles made of Deere skins, & aprons of the fame rounde about their middles; all els naked; of fuch a difference of ftatures only as wee in England; hauing no edge tooles or weapons of yron or fteele to offend vs withall, neither know they how to make any: thofe weapós that they haue, are onlie bowes made of Witch hazle, & arrowes of reeds; flat edged truncheons alfo of wood about a yard long, neither haue they any thing to defend themfelues but targets made of barcks; and fome armours made of ftickes wickered together with thread.

Their townes are but fmall, & neere the fea coaft but few, fome cótaining but 10. or 12. houfes: fome 20. the greateft that we haue feene haue bene but of 30. houfes: if they be walled it is only done with barks of trees made faft to ftakes, or els with poles onely fixed vpright and clofe one by another.

Their houfes are made of fmall poles made faft at the tops in rounde forme after the maner as is vfed in many arbories in our gardens of England, in moft townes couered with barkes, and in fome with artificiall mattes made of long rushes; from the tops of the houfes downe to the ground. The length of them is commonly double to the breadth, in fome places they are but 12. and 16. yardes long, and in other fome wee haue feene of foure and twentie.

In

In some places of the countrey one onely towne belongeth to the governe-
ment of a *Wiróans* or chiefe Lorde; in other some two or three, in some sixe, eight,
& more; the greatest *Wiróans* that yet we had dealing with had but eighteene townes in his governmēt, and able to make not aboue seuen or eight hundred fighting
men at the most: The language of euery gouernment is different from any other,
and the farther they are distant the greater is the difference.

Their maner of warres amongst themselues is either by sudden surprising on
an other most commonly about the dawning of the day, or moone light; or eis by
ambushes, or some suttle deuises: Set battels are very rare, except it fall out where
there are many trees, where cyther part may haue some hope of defence, after the
deliuerie of euery arrow, in leaping behind some or other.

If there fall out any warres betweē vs & them, what their fight is likely to bee,
we hauing aduantages against them so many maner of waies, as by our discipline,
our strange weapons and deuises els; especially by ordinance great and small, it may
be easily imagined; by the experience we haue had in some places, the turning vp
of their heeles against vs in running away was their best defence.

In respect of vs they are a people poore, and for want of skill and iudgement
in the knowledge and vse of our things, doe esteeme our trifles before thinges of
greater value: Notwithstanding in their proper manner considering the want of
such meanes as we haue, they seeme very ingenious; For although they haue no
such tooles, nor any such craftes, sciences and artes as wee; yet in those thinges they
doe, they shewe excellencie of wit. And by howe much they vpon due consideration shall finde our manner of knowledges and craftes to exceede theirs in perfe-
ction, and speed for doing or execution, by so much the more is it probable that
they shoulde desire our friendships & loue, and haue the greater respect for plea-
sing and obeying vs. Whereby may bee hoped if meanes of good gouernment bee
vsed, that they may in short time be brought to ciuilitie, and the imbracing of true
religion.

Some religion they haue alreadie, which although it be farre from the truth,
yet beyng at it is, there is hope it may bee the easier and sooner reformed.

They beleeue that there are many Gods which they call *Mantóac*, but of different sortes and degrees; one onely chiefe and great God, which hath bene from
all eternitie. Who as they affirme when hee purposed to make the worlde, made
first other goddes of a principall order to bee as meanes and instruments to bee v-
sed in the creation and gouernment to follow; and after the Sunne, Moone, and
Starres, as pettie goddes and the instruments of the other order more principall.
First they say were made waters, out of which by the gods was made all diuersitie
of creatures that are visible or inuisible.

For mankind they say a woman was made first, which by the woorking of one
of the goddes, conceiued and brought foorth children: And in such sort they say
they had their beginning.

C 3

But how manie yeeres or ages haue paſſed ſince, they ſay they can make no relation, hauing no letters nor other ſuch meanes as we to keepe recordes of the particularities of times paſt, but onelie tradition from father to ſonne.

They thinke that all the gods are of humane shape, & therfore they repreſent
them by images in the formes of men, which they call *Kewaſowok* one alone is called *Kewás*; Them they place in houſes appropriate or temples which they call
Mathicómuck; Where they woorship, praie, ſing, and make manie times offerings
vnto them. In ſome *Machicómuck* we haue ſeene but on *Kewas*, in ſome two, and
in other ſome three; The common ſort thinke them to be alſo gods.

They beleeue alſo the immortalitie of the ſoule, that after this life as ſoone as
the ſoule is departed fiom the bodie according to the workes it hath done, it is eyther carried to heauē the habitacle of gods, there to enioy perpetuall bliſſe and hap-
pineſſe, or els to a great pitte or hole, which they thinke to bee in the furtheſt partes
of their part of the worlde towarde the ſunne ſet, there to burne continually: the
place they call *Popoguſſo*.

For the confirmation of this opinion, they tolde mee two ſtories of two men
that had been lately dead and reuiued againe, the one happened but few yeres before our comming in the countrey of a wicked man which hauing beene dead and
buried, the next day the earth of the graue beeing ſeene to moue, was takē vp againe; Who made declaration where his ſoule had beene, that is to ſaie very neere en-
tring into *Popoguſſo*, had not one of the gods ſaued him & gaue him leaue to returne againe, and teach his friends what they should doe to auoid that terrible place of
tormenr.

The other happened in the ſame yeere wee were there, but in a towne that was
threeſcore miles from vs, and it was tolde mee for ſtraunge newes that one beeing
dead, buried and taken vp againe as the firſt, shewed that although his bodie had
lien dead in the graue, yet his ſoule was aliue, ānd had trauailed farre in a long broade waie, on both ſides whereof grewe moſt delicate and pleaſaūt trees, bearing more rare and excellent fruites then euer hee had ſeene before or was able to expreſſe,
and at length came to moſt braue and faire houſes, neere which hee met his father,
that had beene dead before, who gaue him great charge to goe backe againe and
shew his friendes what good they were to doe to enioy the pleaſures of that place,
which when he had done he should after come againe.

What ſubtilty ſoeuer be in the *Wiroances* and Prieſtes, this opinion worketh ſo
much in manie of the common and ſimple ſort of people that it maketh them haue great reſpect to their Gouernours, and alſo great care what they do, to auoid tor-
ment after death, and to enioy bliſſe; althought notwithſtanding there is punish-
ment ordained for malefactours, as ſtealers, whoremoongers, and other ſortes of
wicked doers; ſome punished with death, ſome with forfeitures, ſome with beating,
according to the greatnes of the factes.

And this is the ſumme of their religion, **which I** learned by hauing ſpecial fa-
miliarity

miliarity with fome of their prieftes. Wherein they were not fo fure grounded, nor gaue fuch credite to their traditions and ftories but through conuerfing with vs they were brought into great doubts of their owne, and no fmall admiratiõ of ours, with earneft defire in many, to learne more than we had meanes for want of perfect vtterance in their language to expreffe.

Moft thinges they fawe with vs, as Mathematicall inftruments, fea compaffes, the vertue of the loadftone in drawing yron, a perfpectiue glaffe whereby was shewed manie ftrange fightes, burning glaffes, wildefire woorkes, gunnes, bookes, writing and reading, fpring clocks that feeme to goe of themfelues, and manie other thinges that wee had, were fo ftraunge vnto them, and fo farre exceeded their capacities to comprehend the reafon and meanes how they should be made and done, that they thought they were rather the works of gods then of men, or at the leaftwife they had bin giuen and taught vs of the gods. Which made manie of them to haue fuch opinion of vs, as that if they knew not the trueth of god and religion already, it was rather to be had from vs, whom God fo fpecially loued then from a people that were fo fimple, as they found themfelues to be in comparifon of vs. Whereupon greater credite was giuen vnto that we fpake of concerning fuch matters.

Manie times and in euery towne where I came, according as I was able, I made declaration of the contentes of the Bible; that therein was fet foorth the true and onelie G O D, and his mightie woorkes, that therein was contayned the true doctrine of faluation through Chrift, with manie particularities of Miracles and chiefe poyntes of religion, as I was able then to vtter, and thought fitte for the time. And although I told them the booke materially & of it felf was not of anie fuch vertue, as I thought they did conceiue, but onely the doctrine therein cõtained; yet would many be glad to touch it, to embrace it, to kiffe it, to hold it to their brefts and heades, and ftroke ouer all their bodie with it; to shewe their hungrie defire of that knowledge which was fpoken of.

The *Wiroans* with whom we dwelt called *Wingina*, and many of his people would be glad many times to be with vs at our praiers, and many times call vpon vs both in his owne towne, as alfo in others whither he fometimes accompanied vs, to pray and fing Pfalmes; hoping thereby to bee partaker of the fame effectes which wee by that meanes alfo expected.

Twife this *Wiroans* was fo grieuoufly ficke that he was like to die, and as hee laie languishing, doubting of anie helpe by his owne prieftes, and thinking he was in fuch daunger for offending vs and thereby our god, fent for fome of vs to praie and bee a meanes to our God that it would pleafe him either that he might liue or after death dwell with him in bliffe, fo likewife were the requeftes of manie others in the like cafe

On a time alfo when their corne began to wither by reafon of a drouth which happened extraordinarily, fearing that it had come to paffe by reafon that in fome thing they had difpleafed vs, many woulde come to vs & defire vs to praie to our God of England, that he would preferue their corne, promifing that when it was ripe we alfo should be partakers of the fruite.

There could at no time happen any ftrange fickneffe, loffes, hurtes, or any other croffe vnto them, but that they would impute to vs the caufe or meanes therof for offending or not pleafing vs.

One other rare and ftrange accident, leauing others, will I mention before I ende, which mooued the whole countrey that either knew or hearde of vs, to haue vs in wonderfull admiration.

There was no towne where we had any fubtile deuife practifed againft vs, we leauing it vnpunished or not reuenged (becaufe wee fought by all meanes poffible to win them by gentleneffe) but that within a few dayes after our departure from euerie fuch towne, the people began to die very faft, and many in short fpace; in fome townes about twentie, in fome fourtie, in fome fixtie, & in one fixe fcore, which in trueth was very manie in refpect of their numbers. This happened in no place that wee coulde learne but where wee had bene, where they vfed fome practife againft vs, and after fuch time; The difeafe alfo fo ftrange, that they neither knew what it was, nor how to cure it; the like by report of the oldeft men in the countrey neuer happened before, time out of minde. A thing fpecially obferued by vs as alfo by the naturall inhabitants themfelues.

Infomuch that when fome of the inhabitants which were our friends & efpecially the *Wiroans Wingina* had obferued fuch effects in foure or fiue towns to follow their wicked practifes, they were perfwaded that it was the worke of our God through our meanes, and that wee by him might kil and flai whom wee would without weapons and not come neere them.

And thereupon when it had happened that they had vnderftanding that any of their enemies had abufed vs in our iourneyes, hearing that wee had wrought no reuenge with our weapons, & fearing vpon fome caufe the matter should fo reft: did come and intreate vs that we woulde bee a meanes to our God that they as others that had dealt ill with vs might in like fort die ; alleaging howe much it would be for our credite and profite, as alfo theirs; and hoping furthermore that we would do fo much at their requefts in refpect of the friendship we profeffe them.

Whofe entreaties although wee shewed that they were vngodlie, affirming that our God would not fubiect him felfe to anie fuch praiers and requeftes of mē: that in deede all thinges haue beene and were to be done according to his good pleafure as he had ordained : ād that we to shew our felues his true feruāts ought rather to make petition for the contrarie, that they with them might liue together with vs, bee made partakers of his truth & ferue him in righteoufnes ; but notwithftanding in fuch fort, that wee referre that as all other thinges, to bee done according to his diuine will & pleafure, ād as by his wifedome he had ordained to be beft.

Yet

Yet becaufe the effect fell out fo fodainly and fhortly after according to their defires, they thought neuerthelefle it came to pafle by our meanes, and that we in vfing fuch fpeeches vnto them did but diflemble the matter, and therefore came vnto vs to giue vs thankes in their manner that although wee fatisfied them not in promife, yet in deedes and effect we had fulfilled their defires.

This maruelous accident in all the countrie wrought fo ftrange opinions of vs, that fome people could not tel whether to think vs gods or men, and the rather becaufe that all the fpace of their ficknefle, there was no man of ours knowne to die, or that was fpecially ficke: they noted alfo that we had no women amongft vs, neither that we did care for any of theirs.

Some therefore were of opinion that wee were not borne of women, and therefore not mortall, but that wee were men of an old generation many yeeres paft then rifen againe to immortalitie.

Some woulde likewife feeme to prophefie that there were more of our generation yet to come, to kill theirs and take their places, as fome thought the purpofe was by that which was already done.

Thofe that were immediatly to come after vs they imagined to be in the aire, yet inuifible & without bodies, & that they by our intreaty & for the loue of vs did make the people to die in that fort as they did by fhooting inuifible bullets into them.

To confirme this opinion their phifitions to excufe their ignorance in curing the difeafe, would not be afhemed to fay, but earneftly make the fimple people beleue, that the ftrings of blood that they fucked out of the ficke bodies, were the ftrings wherewithal the inuifible bullets were tied and caft.

Some alfo thought that we fhot them our felues out of our pieces from the place where we dwelt, and killed the people in any fuch towne that had offended vs as we lifted, how farre diftant from vs foeuer it were.

And other fome faide that it was the fpeciall woorke of God for our fakes, as wee our felues haue caufe in fome forte to thinke no lefle, whatfoeuer fome doe or maie imagine to the contrarie, fpecially fome Aftrologers knowing of the Eclipfe of the Sunne which wee faw the fame yeere before in our voyage thytherward, which vnto them appeared very terrible. And alfo of a Comet which beganne to appeare but a few daies before the beginning of the faid ficknefle. But to exclude them from being the fpeciall an accident, there are farther reafons then I thinke fit at this prefent to bee alleadged.

Thefe their opinions I haue fet downe the more at large that it may appeare vnto you that there is good hope they may be brought through difcreet dealing and gouernement to the imbracing of the trueth, and confequently to honour, obey, feare and loue vs.

d

And although some of our companie towardes the ende of the yeare, shewed themselues too fierce, in slaying some of the people, in some towns, vpo causes that on our part, might easily enough haue been borne withall : yet notwithstanding because it was on their part iustly deserued, the alteration of their opinions generally & for the most part concerning vs is the lesse to bee doubted. And whatsoeuer els they may be, by carefulnesse of our selues neede nothing at all to be feared.

The best neuerthelesse in this as in all actions besides is to be endeuoured and hoped, & of the worst that may happen notice to bee taken with consideration, and as much as may be eschewed.

The

The Conclusion.

Now I haue as I hope made relation not of so fewe and smal things but that the countrey of men that are indifferent & wel disposed maie be sufficiently liked: If there were no more knowen then I haue mentioned, which doubtlesse and in great reason is nothing to that which remaineth to bee discouered, neither the soile, nor commodities. As we haue reason so to gather by the difference we found in our trauails: for although all which I haue before spoken of, haue bin discouered & experimented not far from the sea coast where was our abode & most of our trauailing: yet somtimes as we made our iourneies farther into the maine and countrey; we found the soyle to bee fatter; the trees greater and to growe thinner; the grounde more firme and deeper mould; more and larger champions; finer grasse and as good as euer we saw any in England; in some places rockie and farre more high and hillie ground; more plentie of their fruites; more abondance of beastes; the more inhabited with people, and of greater pollicie & larger dominions, with greater townes and houses.

Why may wee not then looke for in good hope from the inner parts of more and greater plentie, as well of other things, as of those which wee haue alreadie discouered? Vnto the Spaniardes happened the like in discouering the maine of the West Indies. The maine also of this countrey of *Virginia*, extending some wayes so many hundreds of leagues, as otherwise then by the relation of the inhabitants wee haue most certaine knowledge of, where yet no Christian Prince hath any possession or dealing, cannot but yeeld many kinds of excellent commodities, which we in our discouerie haue not yet seene.

What hope there is els to be gathered of the nature of the climate, being answerable to the Iland of *Iapan*, the land of *China*, *Persia*, *Iury*, the Ilandes of *Cyprus* and *Candy*, the South parts of *Greece*, *Italy*, and *Spaine*, and of many other notable and famous countreis, because I meane not to be tedious, I leaue to your owne consideration.

Whereby also the excellent temperature of the ayre there at all seasons, much warmer then in England, and neuer so violently hot, as sometimes is vnder & between the Tropikes, or nere them; cannot bee vnknowne vnto you without farther relation.

For the holsomnesse thereof I neede to say but thus much: that for all the want of prouision, as first of English victuall; excepting for twentie daies, wee liued only by drinking water and by the victuall of the countrey, of which some sorts were very straunge vnto vs, and might haue bene thought to haue altered our temperatures in such sort as to haue brought vs into some greeuous and dagerous diseases: secondly the wāt of English meanes, for the taking of beastes, fishe, and foule, which by the helpe only of the inhabitants and their meanes, coulde not bee so suddenly and eafily prouided for vs, nor in fo great numbers & quantities, nor of that choife as otherwife might haue bene to our better fatisfaction and contentment. Some want alfo wee had of clothes. Furthermore, in all our trauailes which were moft fpeciall and often in the time of winter, our lodging was in the open aire vpon the grounde. And yet I fay for all this, there were but foure of our whole company (being one hundred and eight) that died all the yeere and that but at the latter ende thereof and vpon none of the aforefaide caufes. For all foure efpecially three were feeble, weake, and fickly perfons before euer they came thither, and thofe that knewe them much marueyled that they liued fo long beeing in that cafe, or had aduentured to trauaile.

Seing therefore the ayre there is fo temperate and holfome, the foyle fo fertile and yeelding fuch commodities as I haue before mentioned, the voyage alfo thither to and fro beeing fufficiently experimented, to bee perfourmed thrife a yeere with eafe and at any feafon thereof: And the dealing of Sir *Water Raleigh* fo liberall in large giuing and graũting lande there, as is alreadie knowen, with many helpes and furtherances els: (The leaft that hee hath graunted hath beene fiue hundred acres to a man onely for the aduenture of his perfon:) I hope there remaine no caufe wherby the action should be mifliked.

If that thofe which shall thiter trauaile to inhabite and plant bee but reafonably prouided for the firft yere as thofe are which were tranfported the laft, and beeing there doe vfe but that diligence and care as is requifite, and as they may with eefe: There is no doubt but for the time following they may haue victuals that is excellent good and plentie enough; fome more Englishe fortes of cattaile alfo hereafter, as fome haue bene before, and are there yet remaining, may and shall bee God willing thiter tranfported: So likewife our kinde of fruites, rootes, and hearbes may bee there planted and fowed, as fome haue bene alreadie, and proue wel: And in short time alfo they may raife of thofe fortes of commodities which I haue fpoken of as shall both enrich them felues, as alfo others that shall deale with them.

And this is all the fruites of our labours, that I haue thought neceffary to aduertife you of at this prefent: what els concerneth the nature and manners of the inhabitants of *Virginia:* The number with the particularities of the voyages thither made; and of the actions of fuch that haue bene by Sir *Water Raleigh* therein and there imployed, many worthy to bee remembred; as of the firft difcouerers of the Countrey: of our generall for the time Sir *Richard Greinuile*; and after his departure, of our Gouernour there Mafter *Rafe Lane*; with diuers other directed and imployed vnder theyr gouernement: Of the Captaynes and Mafters of the voyages made fince for tranfportation; of the Gouernour and affiftants of thofe alredie tranfported, as of many perfons, accidẽts, and thinges els, I haue ready in a difcour-

fe by

se by it self in maner of a Chronicle according to the course of times, and when time shall bee thought conuenient shall be also published.

Thus referring my relation to your fauourable constructions, expecting good successe of the action, from him which is to be acknowledged the authour and gouernour not only of this but of all things els, I take my leaue of you, this moneth of Februarii, 1 5 8 8.

F I N I S.

d 3

THE TRVE PICTVRES AND FASHIONS OF THE PEOPLE IN THAT PARTE OF AMERICA NOVV CAL-LED VIRGINIA, DISCOWRED BY ENGLISMEN

sent thither in the years of our Lorde 1585. att the speciall charge and direction of the Honourable SIR WALTER RALEGH Knigt Lord Warden of the stannaries in the duchies of Corenwal and Oxford who therin hath bynne fauored and auctorised by her MAAIESTIE and her let-ters patents.

Translated out of Latin into English by RICHARD HACKLVIT.

DILIGENTLYE COLLECTED AND DRAOW-ne by IHON WHITE who was sent thiter speciallye and for the same pur-pose by the said SIR WALTER RALEGH the year abouesaid 1585. and also the year 1588. now cutt in copper and first published by THEODORE de BRY att his wone chardges.

THE TABLE
OF ALL DE PICTV-
RES CONTAINED IN
this Booke of Virginia.

Joudeus a Wingle in.   Theodore de Bry fe.

To the gentle Reader.

Lthough (frendlye Reader) man by his disobedience, we are depriued of those good Gifts wher with he was indued in his creation, yet he was not berefte of wit to prouyde for hym selfe, nor discretion to de- uise things necessarie for his vse, except suche as appartayne to his soules healthe, as may be gathered by this sauage nations, of whome this present worke intreateth. For aithough they haue noe true knoledge of God nor of his holye worde and are destituted of all lerninge, Yet they passe vs in many thinges, as in Sober feedinge and Dexteritye of witte, in makinge without any instrument of mettall thinges so neate and so fine, as a man would scarsclye beleue thesame, Vnless the Englishemen Had made proofe Therof by their trauailes into the contrye. Consideringe, Therfore that yt was a thinge worthie of admiration, I was verye willinge to offer vnto you the true Pi- ctures of those people wich by the helfe of Maister Richard Hakluyt of Oxford Mi- nister of Gods Word, who first Incouraged me to publish the Worke, I creaued out of the verye original of Maister Ihon White an Englisch paynter who was sent into the contrye by the queenes Maiestye, onlye to draw the description of the place, lynelye to describe the shapes of the Inhabitants their apparell, manners of Liuinge, and fashions, att the speciall Charges of the worthy knighte, Sir W A L T E R R A- L E G H, who bestowed noe Small Sume of monnye in the serche and Discouerye of that countrye, From te yeers, 1 5 8 4. to the ende of The years 1 5 8 8. Morouer this booke which intreateth of that parte of the new World which the Englishemen call by the name of Virginia I heer sett out in the first place, beinge therunto requested of my Frends, by Raeson of the memorye of the fresh and laue performance ther of, albeyt I haue in hand the Historye of Florida wich should bee first sett foorthe be- cause yt was discouured by the Frencheman longe befor the discouerye of Virginia, yet I hope shortlye also to publish thesame, A Victorye, doubtless so Rare, as I thinke the like hath not ben heard nor seene. I craeued both of them at London, an brought, Them hither to Franckfurt, wher I and my sonnes hauen taken ernest paynes in gra- uinge the pictures ther of in Copper, seeing yt is a matter of noe small importance. Touchinge the stile of both the Discourses, I haue caused yt to bee Reduced into verye Good Frenche and Latin by the aide of verye worshipfull frend of myne. Fi- nallye I hartlye Request thee, that yf any seeke to Contrefaict thes my bookx, (for in this dayes many are so malicious that they seeke to gayne by other men labours) thow wouldest giue noe credit vnto suche conterfaited Drawghte. For dyuers secret marks lye hiddin in my pictures, which wil breede Con- fusion vnless they bee well obserued.

V
N
I
N
SECO
TAN

Mongoack

Cwareuuoc

Panauuaioc

Neuustooc

Sectuooc

Secota

Cotan

Aguscogoc

Paquwyp

Pomeiock

Tramasquec

Dasamonquepe

Promontorium tremendum

Wokokon

Croatoan

Paquiwoc

Hator

Mequope

Mo

Ta

Autore Ioanne With Sculptore Theodore de Bry, Qui et excud

Scala leucarum 25

5   10   15   20   25

Scalle of ·25· leages

CHAWA

RINGOIA

NGOKA

R I O R A
 I

Ramushouua

Ohaunoock

uc
Letocuuen

Catokinge

Waratan

Mascoming

WEAPE

Skicoak

Chepanuu MEOC

Chepanuu

Chesepiooc

Chesepiooc sinus

Comokee

Apasus

Pasquenoke

Trinety harbor

OCCIDENS

MERIDIES

ORIENS

SEPTENTRIO

THe sea coasts of Virginia arre full of Ilãds, wehr by the entrance into the mayne lãd is hard to finde. For although they bee separated with diuers and sundrie large Diuision, which seeme to yeeld conuenient entrance, yet to our great perill we proued that they wear shallowe, and full of dangerous flatts, and could neuer perce opp into the mayne lãd, vntill wee made trialls in many places with or small pinneß. At lengthe wee fownd an entrance vppon our mens diligent serche therof Affter that wee had passed opp, and sayled ther in for a short space we discouered a migthye riuer fallnige downe in to the sownde ouer against those Ilands, which neuerthelesswee could not saile opp any thinge far by Reason of the shallewnes, the mouth ther of beinge annoyed with sands driuen in with the tyde therfore saylinge further, wee came vnto a Good bigg yland, the Inhabitante therof as soone as they saw vs began to make a great an horrible crye, as people which meuer befoer had seene men apparelled like vs, and camme a way makinge out crys like wild beasts or men out of their wyts. But beenge gentlye called backe, wee offred thẽ of our wares, as glasses, kniues, babies, and other trifles, which wee thougt they dcligted in. Soe they stood still, and perceuinge our Good will and courtesie came fawninge vppon vs, and bade us welcome. Then they brougt vs to their village in the iland called, Roanoac, and vnto their Weroans or Prince, which entertained vs with Reasonable curtesie, althoug the wear amased at the first sight of vs. Suche was our arriuall into the parte of the world, which we call Virginia, the stature of bodee of wich people, theyr attire, and maneer of lyuinge, their feasts, and banketts, I will particullerlye declare vnto yow.

THe Princes of Virginia are attyred in suche manner as is expressed in this figure. They weare the haire of their heades long and bynde opp the ende of thesame in a knot vnder thier eares. Yet they cutt the topp of their heades from the forehead to the nape of the necke in manner of a cokscombe, stirkinge a faier lóge pecher of some berd att the Begininge of the creste vppun their foreheads, and another short one on bothe seides about their eares. They hange at their eares ether thicke pearles, or somwhat els, as the clawe of some great birde, as cometh in to their fansye. Moreouer They ether pownes, or paynt their forehead, cheeks, chynne, bodye, armes, and leggs, yet in another sorte then the inhabitantz of Florida. They weare a chaine about their necks of pearles or beades of copper, wich they muche esteeme, and ther of wear they also braselets ohn their armes. Vnder their brests about their bellyes appeir certayne spotts, whear they vse to lett them selues bloode, when they are sicke. They hange before thé the skinne of some beaste verye feinelye dresset in suche sorte, that the tayle hangeth downe behynde. They carye a quiuer made of small rushes holding their bowe readie bent in on hand, and an arrowe in the other, radie to defend themselues. In this manner they goe to warr, or tho their solemne feasts and banquetts. They take muche pleasure in huntinge of deer wher of theris great store in the contrye, for yt is fruitfull, pleasant, and full of Goodly woods. Yt hathe also store of riuers full of diuers sorts of fishe. When they go to battel they paynt their bodyes in the moste terible manner that thei can deuise.   A

He woemé of Secotam are of Reaſonable good proportion. In their goinge they
carrye their háds danglinge downe, and air dadil in a deer skinne verye excellétlye
wel dreſſed, hanginge downe frô their nauell vnto the mydds of their thighes, which
alſo couereth their hynder partz. The reſte of their bodies are all bare. The forr parte
of their haire is cutt ſhorte, the reſt is not ouer Longe, thinne, and ſofte, and falling
downe about their ſhoulders: They weare a Wrrath about their heads.   Their foreheads, cheeks,
chynne, armes and leggs are pownced.   About their necks they wear a chaine, ether pricked or
paynted. They haue ſmall eyes, plaine and flatt noſes, narrow foreheads, and broade mowths.   For
the moſt parte they hange at their eares chaynes of longe Pearles, and of ſome ſmootht bones.
Yet their nayles are not longe, as the woemen of Florida.   They are alſo deligtted
with walkinge in to the fields, and beſides the riuers, to ſee the
huntinge of deers and catchinge of
fiſche.

A   2

On of the Religeous men in the   V.
towne of Secota.

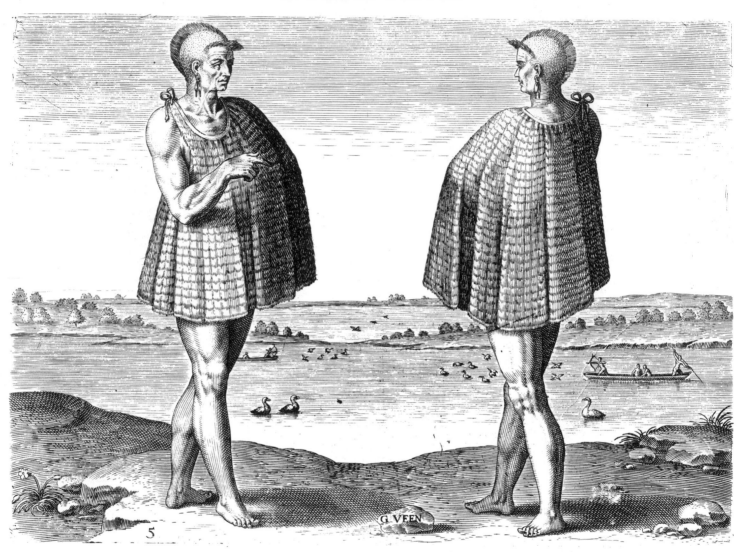

THe Priefts of the aforefaid **Towne of Secota** are well ftricken in yeers, and as yt fee-meth of more experience then the comon forte. They weare their heare cutt like a crefte, on the topps of thier heades as other doe, but the reft are cutt fhorte, fauinge thofe which growe aboue their foreheads in manner of a perriwigge. They alfo ha-ue fomwhat hanginge in their ears. They weare a fhorte clocke made of fine hares skinnes quilted with the hayre outwarde. The reft of thier bodie is naked. They are notable enchaunters, and for their pleafure they frequent the riuers, to kill with their bowes, and catche wilde ducks, fwannes, and other fowles.

A younge gentill woeman doughter VI.
of Secota.

6   G·VEEN

VIrgins of good parentage are apparelled altogether like the woemen of Secota aboue mentionned, sauing that they weare hanginge abowt their necks in steede of a chaine certaine thicke, and rownde pearles, with little beades of copper, or polished bones betweene them. They pounce their foreheads, cheeckes, armes and legs. Their haire is cutt with two ridges aboue their foreheads, the rest is trussed opp on a knott behinde, they haue broade mowthes, reasonable fair black eyes: they lay their hands often vppon their Shoulders, and couer their brests in token of maydenlike modestye. The rest of their bodyes are naked, as in the picture is to bee seene.
They deligt also in seeinge fishe taken in
the riuers.

A   4

A cheiff Lorde of Roanoac. VII.

He cheefe men of the yland and towne of Roanoac reace the haire of their crounes of theyr heades cutt like a cokes côbe, as the other doe. The reft they wear lôge as woemen and trufs them opp in a knott in the nape of their necks. They hange pearles ftringe oppon a threed att their eares, and weare bracelets on their armes of pearles, or fmall beades of copper or of fmoothe bone called minfal, nether painptinge nor powncings of them felues, but in token of authoritye, and honor, they wear a chaine of great pearles, or copper beades or fmoothe bones abowt their necks, and a plate of copper hinge vpon a ftringe, from the nauel vnto the midds of their thighes. They couer themfelues before and behynde as the woemé doe with a deers skynne handfomley dreffed, and fringed, More ouer they fold their armes together as they walke, or as they talke one wjth another in figne of wifdome.
The yle of Roanoac is verye pleifant, ond hath plaintie of fifhe by reafon of the Water that enuironeth thefame.

T·B·   8

About 20. milles from that Iland, neere the lake of Paquippe, ther is another towne called Pomeioock hard by the fea. The apparell of the cheefe ladyes of dat towne differeth but litle from the attyre of thofe which lyue in Roanaac. For they weare their haire truffed opp in a knott, as the maiden doe which we fpake of before, and haue their fkinnes pownced in thefame manner, yet they wear a chaine of great pearles, or beades of copper, or fmoothe bones 5. or 6. fold obout their necks, be-aringe one arme in the fame, in the other hand they carye a gourde full of fome kinde of pleafant liquor. They tye deers fkinne doubled about them crochinge hygher about their breafts, which hange downe before almoft to their knees, and are almoft altogither naked behinde. Commonlye their yonge daugters of 7. or 8. yeares olde do waigt vpon them wearinge abowt them a girdle of fkinne, which hangeth downe behinde, and is drawen vnder neath betwene their twifte, and bown-de aboue their nauel with mofe of trees betwene that and thier fkinnes to couer their priuiliers withall. After they be once paft 10. yeares of age, they wear deer fkinnes as the older forte do.
They are greatlye Diligted with puppetts, and babes which wear brought oute of England.

An ageed manne in his winter IX.
garment.

He aged men of Pommeioocke are couered with a large skinne which is tyed vppon their shoulders on one side and hangeth downe beneath their knees wearinge their other arme naked out of the skinne, that they maye bee at more libertie. Those skynnes are Dressed with the hair on, and lyned with other furred skinnes. The yonnge men suffer noe hairr at all to growe vppon their faces but assoone as they growe they put them away, but when thy are come to yeeres they suffer them to growe although to say truthe they come opp verye thinne. They also weare their haire bownde op behynde, and, haue a creste on their heads like the others. The contrye abowt this plase is soe fruit full and good, that England is not to bee compared to yt.

B

Their manner of careynge ther Chil- X.
dern and a tyere of the cheiffe Ladyes of the
towne of Dasamonquepeuc.

I N the towne of Dasemonquepeuc distant from Roanoac 4. or 5. milles, the woemen are attired, and pownced, in suche sorte as the woemen of Roanoac are, yet
they weare noe worathes vppon their heads, nether haue they their thighes painted
with small pricks. They haue a strange manner of bearing their children, and quite
contrarie to ours. For our woemen carrie their children in their armes before
their brests, but they taking their sonne by the right hand, bear him on their backs,
holdinge the left thighe in their lefte arme after a strange, and conuesnall fashion, as in the picture is
to bee seene.

B 2

Hey haue comonlye coniurers or iuglers which vſe ſtrange geſtures, and often cōtrarie to nature in their enchantments: For they be verye familiar with deuils, of whome they enquier what their enemys doe, or other ſuche thinges. They ſhaue all their heads ſauinge their creſte which they weare as other doe, and faſten a ſmall black birde aboue one of their ears as a badge of their office. They weare nothinge but a ſkinne which hangeth downe from their gyrdle, and couereth their priuityes. They weare a bagg by their ſide as is expreſſed in the figure. The Inhabitants giue great credit vnto their ſpeeche, which oftentymes they finde to bee true.

B 3

The manner of makinge their boates. XII.

He manner of makinge their boates in Virginia is verye wonderfull. For wheras they want Inſtruments of yron, or other like vnto ours, yet they knowe howe to make them as handſomelye, to ſaile with whear they liſte in their Riuers, and to fiſhe with all, as ours. Firſt they chooſe ſome longe, and thicke tree, accordinge to the bignes of the boate which they would frame, and make a fyre on the grownd abowt the Roote therof, kindlinge the ſame by little, and little with drie moſſe of trees, and chipps of woode that the flame ſhould not mounte opp to highe, and burne to muche of the lengte of the tree. When yt is almoſt burnt thorough, and readye to fall they make a new fyre, which they ſuffer to burne vntill the tree fall of yt owne accord. Then burninge of the topp, and bowghs of the tree in ſuche wyſe that the bodie of theſame may Retayne his iuſt lengthe, they raiſe yt vppon potes laid ouer croſſ wiſe vppon forked poſts, at ſuche a reaſonable heighte as rhey may handſomlyc worke vppó yt. Then take they of the barke with certayne ſhells: thy reſerue the, innermoſt parte of the lennke, for the nethermoſt parte of the boate. On the other ſide they make a fyre accordinge to the lengthe of the bodye of the tree, ſauinge at both the endes. That which they thinke is ſufficientlye burned they quenche and ſcrape away with ſhells, and makinge a new fyre they burne yt agayne, and ſoe they continne ſomtymes burninge and ſometymes ſcrapinge, vntill the boate haue ſufficient bothowmes. This god indueth thiſe ſauage people with ſufficient reaſon to make thinges neceſſarie to ſerue their turnes.

XIII.

Their manner of fishynge in Virginia.

Hey haue likewife a notable way to catche fishe in their Riuers. for whear as they lacke both yron, and steele, they faste vnto their Reedes or longe Rodds, the hollowe tayle of a certaine fishe like to a sea crabb in steede of a poynte, wehr with by nighte or day they stricke fishes, and take them opp into their boates. They also know how to vfe the prickles, and pricks of other fishes. They also make weares, with settinge opp reedes or twigges in the water, which they foe plant one within a nother, that they growe still narrower, and narrower, as appeareth by this figure. Ther was neuer seene amonge vs foe cunninge a way to take fish withall, wherof fondrie fortes as they fownde in their Riuers vnlike vnto ours. which are alfo of a verye good tafte. Dowbtlefs yt is a pleafant fighte to fee the people, fomtymes wadinge, and goinge fomtymes failinge in thofe Riuers, which are shallowe and not deepe, free from all care of heapinge opp Riches for their posterite, content with their state, and liuinge frendlye together of thofe thinges which god of his bountye hath giuen vnto them, yet without giuinge hym any thankes according to his defarte.

So fauage is this people, and depriued of the true knowledge of god.
For they haue none other then is mentionned before in this worke.

The brovvyllinge of their fiſhe XIIII.
ouer the flame.

AFter they haue taken ſtore of fiſhe, they gett them vnto a place fitt to dreſs yt. Ther they ſticke vpp in the grownde 4. ſtakes in a ſquare roome, and lay 4 potes vppon them, and others ouer thwart theſame like vnto an hurdle, of ſufficient heigthe. and layinge their fiſhe vppon this hurdle, they make a fyre vnderneathe to broile the ſame, not after the manner of the people of Florida, which doe but ſchorte, and harden their meate in the ſmoke onlye to Reſerue theſame duringe all the winter. For this people reſeruinge nothinge for ſtore, thei do broile, and ſpend away all att once and when they haue further neede, they roſte or ſeethe freſh, as wee ſhall ſee heraffter. And when as the hurdle can not holde all the fiſhes, they hange the Reſt by the fyrres on ſticks ſett vpp in the grounde a gainſt the fyre, and than they finiſhe the reſt of their cookerye. They take good heede that they bee not burntt. When the firſt are broyled they lay others on, that weare newlye broughte, continuinge the dreſſinge of their meate in this ſorte, vntill they thincke they haue ſufficient.

Their seetheynge of their meate in   XV.
earthen pottes.

G   VEEN

Heir woemen know how to make earthen veſſells with ſpecial Cunninge and that
ſo large and fine, that our potters with lhoye wheles can make noe better: ant then
Remoue them from place to place as eaſelye as we candoe our braſſen kettles. After they haue ſet them vppon an heape of erthe to ſtay them from fallinge, they
putt wood vnder which being kyndled one of them taketh great care that the ſyre
burne equallye Rounde abowt. They or their woemen fill the veſſel with water,
and then putt they in fruite, fleſh, and fiſh, and lett all boyle together like a galliemaufrye, which
the Spaniarde call, olla podrida. Then they putte yt out into diſches, and ſett before the com-
panye, and then they make good cheere together. Yet are they moderate in their eatinge wher
by they auoide ſicknes. I would to god wee would followe their exemple. For wee ſhould bee
free from many kynes of diſeaſyes which wee fall into by ſumptwous and vnſeaſonable banketts,
continuallye deuiſinge new ſawces, and prouocation of gluttonnye to ſatiſſie
our vnſatiable appetite.

Their ſitting at meate.   XVI.

Heir manner of feeding is in this wiſe. They lay a matt made of bents one the grownde and ſett their meate on the mids therof, and then ſit downe Rownde, the men vppon one ſide, and the woemen on the other. Their meate is Mayz ſodden, in ſuche ſorte as I deſcribed yt in the former treatiſe of verye good taſte, deers fleſche, or of ſome other beaſte, and fiſhe. They are verye ſober in their eatinge, and trinkinge, and conſequentlye verye longe liued becauſe they doe not oppreſs nature.

C

XVII.

Their manner of prainge vvith Rattels abowt te fyer.

VHen they haue escaped any great danger by sea or lande, or be returned from the warr in token of Ioye they make a great fyer abowt which the men, and woemen sist together, holdinge a certaine fruite in their hands like vnto a rownde pompió or a gourde, which after they haue taken out the fruits, and the seedes, then fill with smal stons or certayne bigg kernellt to make the more noise, and fasten that vppon a sticke, and singinge after their manner, they make merrie: as my selfe obserued and noted downe at my beinge amonge them. For it is a strange custome, and worth the obseruation.

XVIII.

Theirdanſes vvhich they vſe att their hyghe feaſtes.

AT a Certayne tyme of the yere they make a great, and ſolemne feaſte whe-runto their neighbours of the townes adioninge re-payre from all parts, euery man attyred in the moſt ſtrange faſhion they can deuiſe hauinge certayne marks on the backs to declare of what place they bee. The place where they meet is a broade playne, abowt the which are planted in the grownde certayne poſts carued with heads like to the faces of Nonnes couered with theyr vayles. Then beeing ſett in order they dance, ſinge, and vſe the ſtrangeſt ge-ſtures that they can poſſiblye deuiſe. Three of the fayreſt Virgins, of the companie are in the mydds, which imbraſſinge one ano-ther doe as yt wear turne abowt in their dancinge. All this is donne after the ſunne is ſett for auoydinge of heate. When they are weerye of dancinge. they goe oute of the circle, and come in vntill their dances be ended,and they goe to make merrye as is expreſſed in the 16. figure.

XIX.

The Tovvne of Pomeiooc.

THe townes of this contrie are in a maner like vnto thofe which are in Florida , yet are they not foe ftronge nor yet preferued with foe great care. They are compaffed abowt with poles ftarcke fafte in the grownd, but they are not verye ftronge. The entrance is verye narrowe as may be feene by this picture, which is made accordinge to the forme of the towne of Pomeiooc. Ther are but few howfes therin, faue thofe which belonge to the kinge and his nobles. On the one fide is their tempel feparated from the other howfes, and marked with the letter A. yt is builded rownde, and couered with skynne matts, and as yt wear compaffed abowt. With cortynes without windowes, and hath noe ligthe but by the doore. On the other fide is the kings lodginge marked with the letter B. Their dwellinges are builded with certaine potes faftened together , and couered with matts which they turne op as high as they thinke good, and foe receue in the lighte and other. Some are alfo couered with boughes of trees, as euery man lufteth or liketh beft. They keepe their feafts and make good cheer together in the midds of the towne as yt is defcribed in they 17. Figure. When the towne ftandeth fare from the water they digg a great poude noted with the letter C. wherhence they fetche as muche water as they neede.

X X.

The Tovvne of Secota.

Heir townes that are not inclosed with poles aire commonlye fayrer. Then suche as are inclosed, as appereth in this figure which liuelye expresseth the towne of Secotam. For the howses are Scattered heer and ther, and they haue gardein expressed by the letter E. wherin groweth Tobacco which the inhabitants call Vppowoc. They haue also groaues wherin thei take deer, and fields vherin they sowe their corne. In their corne fields they builde as yt weare a scaffolde wher on they sett a cottage like to a rownde chaire, signiffied by F. wherin they place one to watche. for there are suche nomber of fowles, and beasts, that vnles they keepe the better watche, they would soone deuoure all their corne. For which cause the watcheman maketh continual cryes and noyse. They sowe their corne with a certaine distance noted by H. other wise one stalke would choke the growthe of another and the corne would not come vnto his rypeurs G. For the leaues therof are large, like vnto the leaues of great reedes. They haue also a seuerall broade plotte C. whear they meete with their neighbours, to celebrate their cheefe solemne feastes as the 18. picture doth declare: and a place D. whear after they haue ended their feaste they make merrie togither. Ouer againste this place they haue a rownd plott B. wher they assemble themselues to make their solemne prayers. Not far from which place ther is a lardge buildinge A. wherin are the tombes of their kings and princes, as will appere by the 22. figure likewise they haue garden notted bey the letter I. wherin they vse to sowe pompions. Also a place marked with K. wherin the make a fyre att their solemne feasts, and hard without the towne a riuer L. from whence they fetche their water. This people therfore voyde of all couetousnes lyue cherfullye and att their harts ease. Butt they solemnise their feasts in the nigt, and therfore they keepe verye great fyres to auoyde darkenes, ant to testifie their Ioye.

TB 20.

He people of this cuntrie haue an Idol, which they call KIWASA: yt is carued of woode in lengthe 4. foote whoſe heade is like the heades of the people of Florida, the face is of a fleſh colour, the breſt white, the reſt is all blacke, the thighes are alſo ſpottet with whitte. He hath a chayne abowt his necke of white beades, betweene which are other Rownde beades of copper which they eſteeme more then golde or ſiluer. This Idol is placed in the temple of the towne of Secotam, as the keper of the kings dead corpſes. Somtyme they haue two of theſ idoles in theyr churches, and ſomtine 3. but neuer aboue, which they place in a darke corner wher they ſhew terrible. Theſ poore ſoules haue none other knowledge of god although I thinke them verye Deſirous to know the truthe. For when as wee kneeled downe on our knees to make our prayers vnto god, they went abowt to imitate vs, and when they ſaw we moued our lipps, they alſo dyd the like. Wherfore that is verye like that they might eaſelye be brongt to the knowledge of the goſpel. God of his mercie grant them this grace.

D 2

XXII.

The Tombe of their Werovvans
or Cheiff Lordes.

He builde a Scaffolde 9. or 10. foote hihe as is expreſſed in this figure vnder the tōbs of theit Weroans, or cheefe lordes which they couer with matts, and lai the dead corpſes of their weroans theruppon in manner followinge. firſt the bowells are taken forthe. Then layinge downe the ſkinne, they cutt all the fleſh cleane from the bones, which the drye in the ſonne, and well dryed the incloſe in Matts, and place at their feete. Then their bones (remaininge ſtill faſtened together with the ligaments whole and vn-corrupted) are couered a gayne with leather, and their carcaſe faſhioned as yf their fleſh wear not taken away. They lapp eache corps in his owne ſkinne after theſame in thus handled, and lay yt in his order by the corpſes of the other cheef lordes. By the dead bodies they ſett their Idol Kiwaſa, wher of we ſpake in the former chapiter: For they are perſuaded that theſame doth kepe the dead bodyes of their cheefe lordes that nothinge may hurt them. Moreouer vnder the foreſaid ſcaffolde ſome on of their preiſts hath his lod-ginge, which Mumbleth his prayers nighte and day, and hath charge of the corpſes. For his bedd he hath two deares ſkinnes ſpredd on the grownde, yf the wether bee cold hee maketh a fyre to warme by withall. Thes poore ſoules are thus inſtructed by natute to reuerence their princes euen after their death.

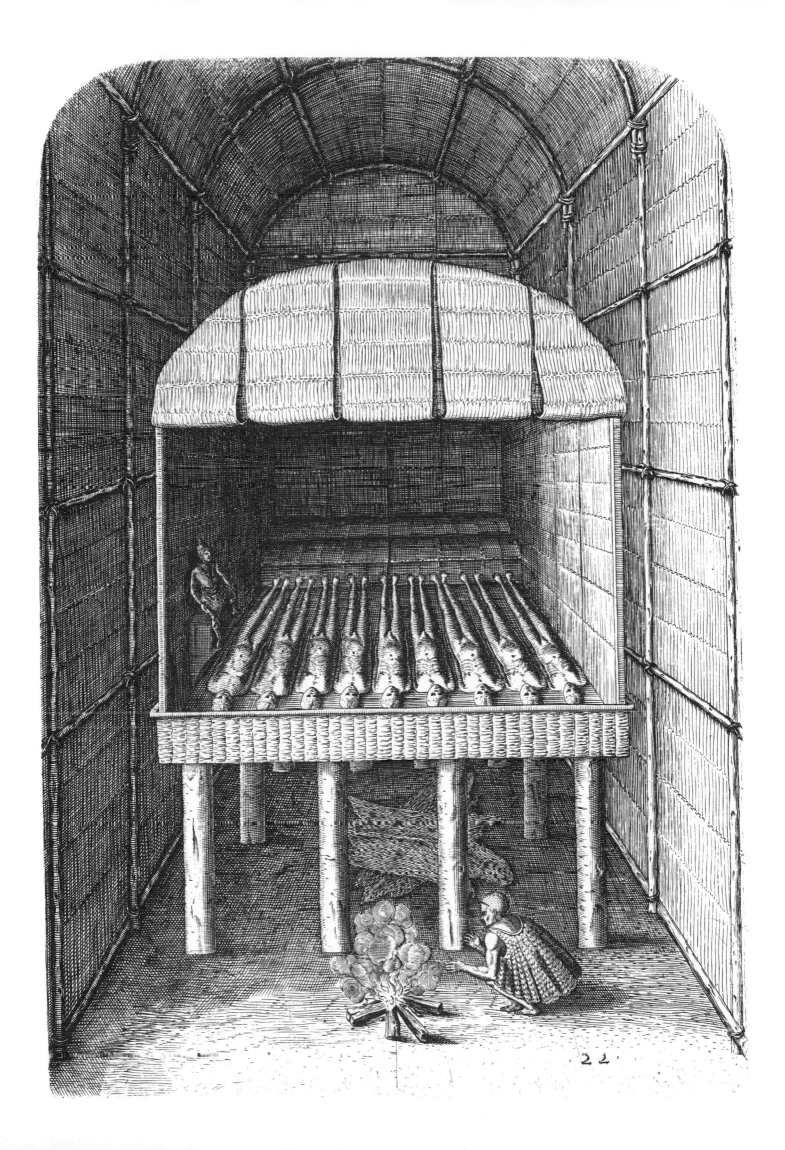

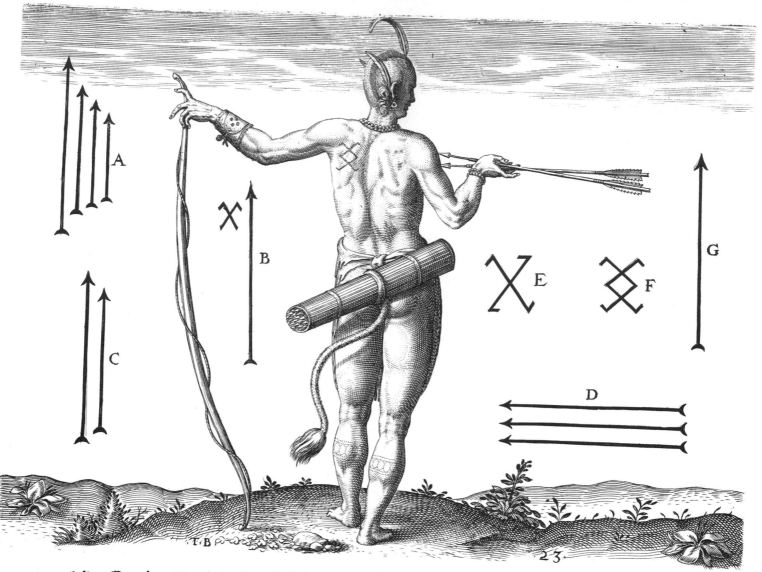

He inhabitãts of all the cuntrie for the most parte haue marks rased on their backs,
wherby yt may be knowen what Princes subiects they bee, or of what place they
haue their originall. For which cause we haue set downe those marks in this figure,
and haue annexed the names of the places, that they might more easelye be discer-
ned. Which industrie hath god indued them withal although they be verye sin-
ple, and rude. And to confesse a truthe I cannot remember, that euer I saw a better
or quietter people then they.

The marks which I obserued a monge them, are heere put downe in order folowinge.

The marke which is expressed by A. belongeth tho Wingino, the cheefe lorde of Roanoac.

That which hath B. is the marke of Wingino his sisters husbande.

Those which be noted with the letters, of C. and D. belonge vnto diuerse chefe lordes in
Secotam.

Those which haue the letters E. F. G. are certaine cheefe men of Pomeiooc, and Aqua-
scogoc.

SOM PICTVRE,
OF THE PICTES
WHICH IN THE OLDE
tyme dyd habite one part of the
great Bretainne.

*THE PAINTER OF WHOM J HAVE
had the firſt of the Inhabitans of Virginia, giue my allſo thees 5. Figures
fallowinge, fownd as hy did aſſured my in a oolld Engliſh cronicle, the which
I wold well ſett to the ende of thees firſt Figures, for to ſhowe how that
the Inhabitants of the great Bretannie haue bin in ti-
mes paſt as ſauuage as thoſe of
Virginia.*

E

The trvve picture of one
Picte I.

IN tymes paſt the Picₜes, habitans of one part of great Bretainne, which is nowe nammed England, wear ſauuages, and did paint all their bodye after the maner followinge. the did lett their haire growe as fare as their Shoulders, ſauinge thoſe which hange vppon their forehead, the which the did cutt. They ſhaue all their berde except the muſtaches, vppon their breaſt wear painted the head of ſom birde, ant about the pappes as yt waere beames of the ſune, vppon the bellye ſum feere full and monſtreus face, ſpreedinge the beames verye fare vppon the thighes. Vppon the tow knees ſom faces of lion, and vppon their leggs as yt hath been ſhelles of fish. Vppon their Shoulders griffones heades, and then they hath ſerpents abowt their armes: They caried abowt their necks one ayerne ringe, and another abowt the midds of their bodye, abowt the bellye, and the ſaids hange on a chaine, a cimeterre or turkie ſoorde, the did carye in one arme a target made of wode, and in the other hande a picke, of which the ayerne was after the manner of a Lick, whith taſſels on, and the other ende with a Rounde boule. And when they hath ouercomme ſome of their ennemis, they did neuer felle to carye a we their heads with them.

The trvve picture of a vvomen
Picte II.

THe woemen of the pictes aboue said wear noe worser for the warres then the men. And wear paynted after the manner followinge, hauinge their heads bear, did lett their hairre flyinge. abowt their Showlders wear painted with griffon heades, the lowe parts and thighes with lion faces, or some other beaste as yt commeth best into their fansye, their brest hath a maner of a half moone, with a great stare, and fowre lesser in booth the sides, their pappes painted in maner of beames of the sonne, and amóg all this a great litteninge starre vppon their brests. The saids of som pointes or beames, and the hoolle bellye as a sonne, the armes, thighes, and leggs well painted, of diuerses Figures: The dyd also carye abowt theyr necks an ayern Ringe, as the men did, and suche a girdle with the soorde hainginge, hauinge a Picke or a lance in one hande, and twoe dardz in the other.

T·B 2

The trvve picture of a yonge
dowgter of the Pictes I I I.

THe yong dougters of the pictes, did alſo lett their haire flyinge, and wear alſo painted ouer all the body, ſo much that noe men could not faynde any different, yf the hath not vſe of another faſhion of paintinge, for the did paint themſelues of ſondrye kinds of flours, and of the faireſt that they cowld feynde. being fourniſhed for the reſt of ſuch kinds of weappon as the woemen wear as you may ſee by this preſent picture a thinge trwelly worthie of admiration.

TB 3

The trvve picture of a man of nation neigbour vnto the Picte I I I I.

Ther was in the said great Bretainne yet another nation nigbour vnto the Pictes, which did apparell them selfues with a kind of cassake other cloath Ierkin, the rest of the bodye wear naked. The did also wear lóge heares, and their moustaches, butt the chin wear also shaued as the other before. The dyd were alardge girdle abowt them, in which hange a croket soorde, with the target, and did carye the picke or the lance in their hande, which hath at the lowe end a rownde bowlle, as you may see by this picture.

The trvve picture of a vvomen
nigbour to the Pictes   V.

Heir woemen wear apparelled after this manner, butt that their apparell was opne before the breſt, and did faſtened with a little leſſe, as our woemen doe faſten their peticott.   They lett hange their breſts outt, as for the reſt the dyd carye ſuche waeppens as the men did, and wear as good as the men for the warre.

A TABLE
OF THE PRINCI-
PALL THINGES THAT
are contained in this Hiſtorie, after the
order of the Alphabet.

F   3

The Table.

The Table.

F I N I S.

*Faults escaped in the impreßion.the first nombre signiffie the
page, the second the Linne.*

Pag.11.lin.22.reade,and. pag.*14*.lin.14.reade sodden. lin.27.reade,about. pag.
16.lin.*19*.reade, sacrifice. pag.20.lin.*18*.reade Discouery. pag.23.li.3. reade hatchets.
In the preface of the figures lin.*17*.reade lyuely.lin.*23*.reade late. figure *2*.lin.*1*.
reade wher.lin.*7*.reade fallinge.lin.10. reade neuer. 18. bodye.

Fig.*3*.lin *5*.reade vppon.fig.7 lin.11 reade and, fig.8.lin.*2*.reade that. fig.*12*.lin.
11.reade they.lin.*16*.reade scrapinge. fig.*13*.lin. 10. reade also.fig.*16*.lin.*6*.drinkinge.
fig.*21*.lin.*12*.about.

The rest if any be the discreete reader may easily amend.

AT FRANCKFORT,
INPRINTED BY IHON WE-
chel, at Theodore de Bry, owne
coaſt and chardges.

M D XC.